THE EMBROIDERED GARDEN

THE EMBROIDERED GARDEN

*Stitching through the Seasons
of a Flower Garden*

Kazuko Aoki

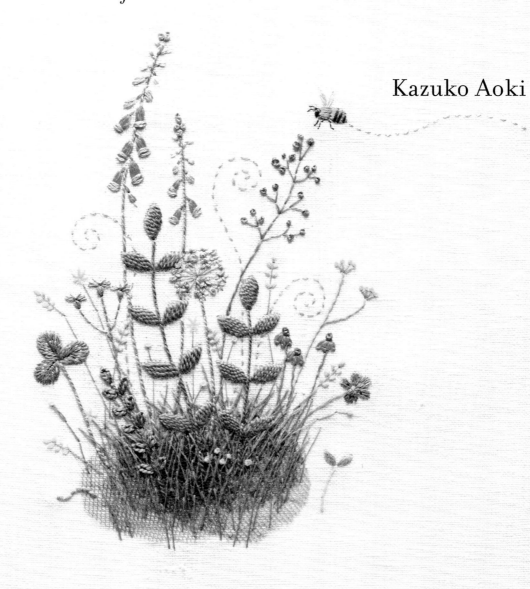

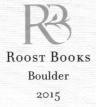

Roost Books

Boulder

2015

CONTENTS

INTRODUCTION

The garden work that begins with herbs and annuals in spring quickly becomes overtaken in the heat of summer by roses and clematis before gradually transforming into a greener and greener garden scape. My feelings about the garden never change, but the garden itself is different every year.

In spring, the bulbs gently sprout and the leaves bud; then, the flowers bloom and bear fruit. This is, of course, evidence that the plants and flowers are living things. Even within the confines of my little garden, the workings of life are constantly evolving. It is a time and space rich with botanical energy. In addition to this, another world of insects and birds descends on my garden. My interest in the garden knows no end.

All along, I've kept a diary of my work in the garden and the flowers that bloom throughout each season. My garden diary is inextricably woven with embroidery, and I hope that those of you who love flowers and gardening will also enjoy this book.

From my atelier,
Kazuko Aoki

SPRING

FOR GARDENERS, THE YEAR BEGINS IN spring. Our spirits are enlivened, as if unfurling in the long-awaited sunshine. We discover shoots from the bulbs we planted in the fall are sprouting from the ground, and we delight in the color schemes of our pansies and violas. Early spring's pinks start with hyacinths and chionodoxa, which are soon followed by tulips. Then the roses appear, and all at once, the garden comes alive with vigor.

SPRING FLOWERS AND SPRING WREATH

Spring Flowers includes red campion, buttercups, daisies, forget-me-nots, mimosa, scilla, and lily of the valley.

For the Spring Wreath, use Indian strawberry vine as a base, then arrange pansies, violas, verbena, ballota, campanula, wood sorrel, daisies, and aegopodium as you like.

HOW TO MAKE PAGES 56 AND 58

GARDEN DIARY

I have been keeping a garden diary since I first started working in my garden. Rather than writing in it every day, the entries are more like memos to myself about which combinations of flowers worked, which seeds I planted, or a list of the roses and clematis I bought that year. As I write, I often have the feeling that I am composing messages to my future self, who will read these next year. Looking over the pages from last year, I see notes that I double-underlined, to make sure I wouldn't overlook them during this year's perusal.

HOW TO MAKE PAGES 62–63

TINY DAISIES

The cover of the garden diary has a full array of tiny
motifs; for this ribbon project, choose a single motif,
or a simple combination, for a small embroidered
design. Wrap the embroidered ribbon around a spool
to make an adorable little stand. Use it for storing
small scissors or plant markers.

HOW TO MAKE PAGE **62**

COLORS OF SPRING

I created a line of fine linen thread, Kazuko Aoki
Original linen thread, dyed in twelve original colors.
In my opinion, linen is the best material to use for
embroidering flowers. It adds a slight matte quality to
the colors and highlights the texture of the stitches.

HOW TO MAKE PAGE 64

MINIATURE GARDEN SKETCH

Create a miniature embroidered garden. The process is exactly the same as if you were gardening: start by preparing the soil (the base); then, proceed with planting, considering the color, shape, and height of the flowers. The beauty of planning an embroidered garden is in its simplicity—you don't have to worry about planting flowers that bloom at different times in nature.

HOW TO MAKE PAGES 64–65

JAM-MAKING SET

Part of the pleasure of making jam is the process itself: adding sugar to the strawberries and simmering it over a low flame, then breathing deep as the sweet smell wafts from the kitchen and permeates the whole house. Preparing the recipe feels like a luxury. With a minimum of effort, these jam jar covers can be used all year long. They are lovely even when made with just scraps of favorite fabric from your stash. And they transform a simple glass jar into a darling present.

HOW TO MAKE PAGES 66–68

BUTTERFLIES
ALL AROUND

In gardening books, I was introduced to the idea
that plants that attracted butterflies were a genus
unto themselves. The butterflies, bees, and various
other insects that flutter by in the garden constitute
their own small world. Here, they are displayed like
specimens.

HOW TO MAKE PAGE 69

BUTTERFLY BROOCH

I made a brooch of one of the cabbage butterflies I've loved since I was a little girl. Even though it's no longer a novelty to me, I still think the lovely design goes well with everything.

HOW TO MAKE PAGE 70

SUMMER

RED AND ORANGE FLOWERS LOOK SO pretty in the blaze of summer sunshine. I have an affinity for blue flowers though, which means that choosing summer blooms is always a source of concern. Using my beloved blue flowers as the center of attention, each year I incorporate a few new colorful additions. The first time I planted globe amaranth, the orange bracts were a surprisingly lovely complement, and their bloom time lasted all summer.

SUMMER FLOWERS AND SUMMER WREATH

Summer Flowers includes aegopodium, globe amaranth, blue salvia, pentas, sunflowers, bluebells, and nicotiana.

For the Summer Wreath, use lippia as a base; then, arrange aegopodium, salvia, clematis, globe amaranth, petunias, zinnias, roses, and pentas as you like.

HOW TO MAKE PAGES 56 AND 59

HERB SAMPLER

Right about the time I started gardening, the practice of growing your own herbs became very popular. I still maintain my fragrant herb garden and use my homegrown stash for cooking. I keep parsley in a flowerpot, and when the time comes around, it serves as a meal for swallowtail caterpillars. I can always buy more parsley, but for the caterpillars, this is all they have, so I don't mind if they eat it up. Yet don't they make a pretty combination of colors? It makes me appreciate the splendor of nature's palette.

HOW TO MAKE PAGES 71–72

LAVENDER SACHET

When I think of fragrant herbs, lavender comes first. Taking inspiration from the herb sampler, I fashioned this sachet. Matching the inner pillow to the color of the embroidery adds sophistication and balance.

HOW TO MAKE PAGES 70–71

GARDENING SET

If you can find gardening gloves made of cloth, embroider them with your own signature motif.

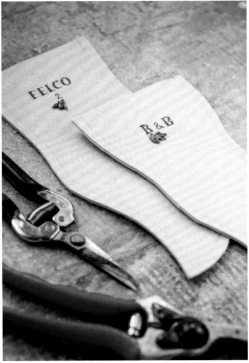

I designed these projects with gardeners, and the various work they do, in mind. For those who have lots of containers, watering is a must, and for those who have many trees, pruning is necessary. My garden has a good amount of trees, roses, and plants. I own many pruners, but the ones I use most are made by the Swiss brand Felco, and for cutting flowers I prefer those made by Burgon & Ball. Hemp twine and plastic ties for securing plants are also essential supplies. Create your own gardening set, including whatever tools you want or need.

HOW TO MAKE PAGES 74–75

SUMMER GARDEN

In the heat of summer I always long to create a shade
garden in the shadow of a big tree. But since summer
is the season for showy flowers to bloom, it's hard to
resist planting some of the most magnificent ones.
I've never grown great mullein (V on the right), but
I've always wanted to try.

HOW TO MAKE PAGES 76–77

AUTUMN

AUTUMN IS THE SEASON WHEN YOU CAN relax and enjoy the flowers in the garden. The plants bear fruit, and, as it gets cooler, the colors of the flowers deepen a shade, becoming that much more beguiling. Plants that made it through summer grow bigger, and when the fall roses are in bloom, the seed packets line the shelves—there have been times when I've had flowers in bloom in every season in the garden. Last to bloom is the Japanese aster. And the one that waits to bloom until the very end is the Mary rose.

AUTUMN FLOWERS AND AUTUMN WREATH

Autumn Flowers includes Japanese aster, meadow sage, tickseed, roses, myrtle, rudbeckia, and mushrooms.
For the Autumn Wreath, use an olive branch and weave in rose hips stalks.

HOW TO MAKE PAGES **57** AND **60**

POCKET BOARD

Once the fruit and berries ripen on the trees and shrubs, the birds arrive. They eat almost all the berries on my myrtle, but they also eat certain insect pests, so I'm willing to turn a blind eye. I don't have blackbirds or robins in my garden, but I've decided that they will make an appearance in this project. For this pocket board, I use corkboard as a base, so memos and notes can be pinned anywhere too.

HOW TO MAKE PAGE 78

BIRD COIN PURSE

A small coin purse is useful in so many ways. Its handy storage space is perfect for little items, of course, but it also works as a card keeper. Make it just a little longer, and it can even hold a compact digital camera. I like to keep a single bird feather tucked away inside— my own little secret.

HOW TO MAKE PAGE 79

SEWING SET

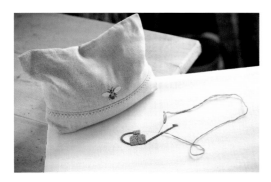

This is a sandbag, used as a weight for embroidery. Place it on the edge of the embroidery frame—now both hands are free, making it much easier to work.

As the nights grow longer, there is more time to do handcrafting. From linen scraps with scalloped edges, make decorative cloth covers for jam jars or coasters too. The best thing about these small projects is that they can be done whenever you can snatch a bit of free time. I find that relaxing with a handmade project not only enriches my daily life but calms my spirit as well. And I like to capture the motifs from the garden that I can't live without and bring them into my needlework.

HOW TO MAKE PAGES 80–81

HOW TO MAKE PAGE 82

GALLERY EXHIBIT

The practice of topiary seems like its own craft within the world of gardening. In the garden, I start a new topiary by coiling the dead undergrowth from false holly around the bottom of a Japanese box tree, and then I use scissors to trim a simple shape, such as a bird. Other shapes I'd like to make are a dress form or a musical clef. But first, I'll create them in embroidery. In these projects, I used my own embroidered floral patches on the dress form.

HOW TO MAKE PAGES 82–84

WINTER

MY FAVORITE THING ABOUT THE WINTER
garden is that nature still brings forth certain
flowers or berries. My table at home is almost always decorated with something from the garden.
Even in deep winter, I can go out and find enough
for a small bouquet.

I've used things like fatsia berry clusters or
modest sarcococca flowers. Most of my long-
lasting Christmas roses are planted in the garden, but I will cut stems from the large base and
use them freely in my arrangements.

WINTER FLOWERS AND WINTER WREATH

Winter Flowers includes fatsia, Christmas rose, narcissus, snowdrops, sarcococca,
and viola.
For the Winter Wreath, use ivy as a base; then, arrange fatsia, flannel flowers,
conifers, and sarcococca as you like.

HOW TO MAKE PAGES 57 AND 61

THROW PILLOWS

For those who call themselves "armchair gardeners," winter is the time of year devoted to planning for the next season from the comfort of a warm home. The garden created in your imagination is abloom with favorite flowers, yet there are no insects to battle and no sun to burn your skin—it's a blissful place. These throw pillows are for those armchair gardeners. Embellish them with whichever kind of frogs you like.

HOW TO MAKE PAGES 86–87

CHRISTMAS ORNAMENTS

All it takes is one or two Christmas decorations to make a home feel festive—that was my inspiration for these ornaments. This wool felt was given to me by Ulla-Karin who owns Östergötlands Ullspinneri in Sweden, and I simply used it as is, embellishing it with a bit of gold embroidery.

HOW TO MAKE PAGES 88–89

EAGERLY AWAITING SPRING

Bulbs that I neglected to plant still put forth a shoot, as I discovered. The green was so fresh and young, it looked like satin ribbon. Bury this handmade bulb in felted wool, and use it as a pincushion. Or arrange green felt to mimic a ball of moss.

HOW TO MAKE PAGE 85

39

Sakuragi

DREAMING OF ROSES

I started my rose garden more than a dozen years ago. Some years, rose-heady days
arrive with almost a hundred stems in bloom at a time. When I see photographs from
back then, the flowers looked to me like clusters of pink, apricot, and white French knots
embroidered on a background of verdant green. After that, I got things in better order
little by little, whittling my rosebushes down to a more manageable number, so that I could
handle them, each on their own. Nevertheless, I still find fascinating new roses that I want
to cultivate or dried-up roses that I want to plant again—there is no end to my rose dreams.

HOW TO MAKE PAGES 90–91

CARD-MAKING

I often come across cute little embroidered objects being sold in shops. Sometimes, they appear to have just a tiny patch stuck on them, so I thought I would try to create card collages that combined a bit of embroidery with little motifs like stamps and such. I came up with combinations of themes and colors, similar and complementary, that I think make the embroidery stand out even more.

HOW TO MAKE PAGES 92–93

GARDENING LIFE
WITH EMBROIDERY

Embroidered Silhouette

HOW TO MAKE PAGE 73

FINDING INSPIRATION FOR EMBROIDERY IN THE GARDEN

Roses are so fragrant in the mornings.
The scent of English roses is captivating.

Sitting on this bench, I'm
surrounded by roses.

Dark colors help to keep things under
control. It's the same way in embroidery.

I never tire of watching the bees—
and I often use them as a motif.

My essential tools for
tending roses.

Observing my garden every day, I notice certain
things. For instance, I know the time of day when
the bees arrive or the spots where various plants
flourish best. Successful combinations of flowers
can often be found later in my embroidery
designs.

By a southern-facing window, I've trained a climbing rose called Alba Meidiland. The pure white clusters of double blooms stand out against the color of the siding of the house. For a bit of variety, I planted medium-sized white iceberg roses in front of the Alba Meidiland. Whether thinking about planting in the garden or about designing embroidery, even though it requires different materials, it seems to me that they use the same part of the brain.

Viewed from inside, the window frames the garden like a work of art. The roses hang down around the window enticingly.

Even the gardening implements become embroidery motifs.

Picking flowers for arrangements also serves to tidy up the beds.

FROM GARDENING TO EMBROIDERY

I gather seasonal flowers and sketch them, deciding the colors when I embroider them. I have found that the shorter the interval from live plants to embroidery is, the more vivid the result will be. I consider what color combinations to use, incorporating balance between different points, lines, and surfaces. For the seasonal wreaths, I arrange the flowers and vines that I've picked from the garden on a plate filled with water, and once I've sketched them, I embroider them.

There is no shortage of motifs to be found in the garden among my favorite plants and the wild grasses that somehow found their place in the mix. The plants may have come from different places or they may have arrived at various times, but once spring comes around, they all grow in together as one to form that year's garden.

I find many gardening books on my travels, which are invaluable resources.

Sketches capture that particular "moment."

I decide on the base for each season's wreath, then I take a walk through the garden to collect plants and flowers, and next I arrange them. At that time, in my mind, I am imagining the surface and lines that the stitches will create. Once I get the materials together for each point of the stitches, then I'm almost finished.

I trace the sketch over and over as I decide what the design will be.

The hardworking honeybees are my companions in embroidery.

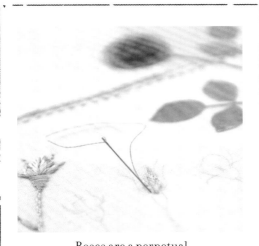

Roses are a perpetual embroidery motif for me.

I stitch with my own line of Kazuko Aoki Original fine linen thread.

I selected twelve colors for my line of linen thread that are perfect for embroidering flowers.

47

EMBROIDERY LIFE WITH GARDENING

Embroidered Silhouette

HOW TO MAKE PAGE 73

KAZUKO'S STITCH LESSONS

MATERIALS AND TOOLS

I'll introduce you to the materials and tools that I always use. There's no need to assemble them all; instead, use them for reference or inspiration. Tools A through H represent the basics you should have on hand.

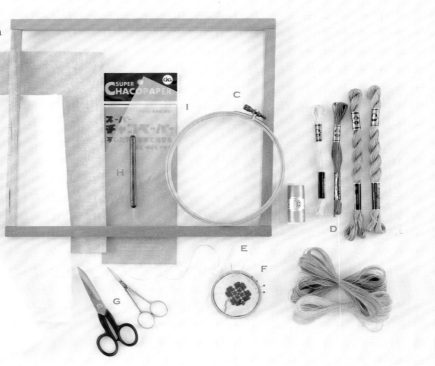

A   Fabric: I often use a stiff linen or linen blend.

B   Fusible Interfacing: When working with a frame, I apply single-sided mid-weight fusible interfacing to the reverse side of the fabric before embroidering.

C   Embroidery Hoop and Frame: For larger projects I use a rectangular frame, and for smaller projects I use a circular hoop. I choose the size that corresponds to each project.

D   Embroidery Floss and Thread: I mainly use DMC embroidery floss, most often DMC No. 25. I use DMC No. 5 for flower stems. For metallic thread, I use DMC Diamant Metallic. And of course, for these projects, I also use my own line of Kazuko Aoki Original linen thread.

E   Embroidery Needles: What I use depends on the weight of the thread and what needles I have available.

F   Marking Pins: I use these to affix a pattern to fabric. I recommend silk pins because they are fine and the heads are small.

G   Scissors: I choose fine-tipped for cutting thread, fabric, and so on.

H   Tracer: This tool is used to trace patterns and transfer them to fabric.

I   Chaco Paper/Tracing Paper: For transferring patterns onto fabric, I choose Chaco paper, because tracing marks can be removed with a damp cloth. I use gray for my designs.

J   Appliqué Fabrics: I use tulle as grass, piecing paper for embroidering on fabric that won't take a traced design, and double-sided fusible interfacing for appliqués. I also use things like gardening "cheesecloth" (coarse, plainly woven, starched fabric).

K   Embellishments: Charms or other such store-bought embroidered patches are perfect as simple accents. For projects that will not be laundered, use paper or other clever materials. Here, I used stamps for the card collages (see page 42).

L   I tried my hand at needle felting for the first time, which uses specialized needles to sculpt balls of wool (page 39). Ribbon embroidery makes projects that much more brilliant with only a little extra work. I use wires as accents in projects (pages 32–33), or I wrap them in thread to make butterfly antennae (page 17).
I use invisible thread when I don't want the thread to be noticed. Carbon transfer paper is useful in overlapping design motifs. I use pliers or nippers to work with wires.

M   I use acrylic paint on fabric when I want to add texture. Letter stamps need just a light hand to work well. These inkpads are designed for use on fabric.

Applying Fusible Interfacing

Most of the time, I apply single-sided midweight fusible interfacing to the reverse side of the fabric. If the swatch is too small, it can be difficult to embroider, so I cut it oversized. Then I trim the interfacing so that it's slightly smaller than the fabric swatch before I iron it evenly, making sure it's securely adhered. I recommend using tracing paper between the iron and the interfacing to avoid getting adhesive on the iron.

Transferring Patterns

1

Copy the pattern onto Chaco paper.

2

Layer in this order: fabric, Chaco paper, pattern, cellophane (it's okay to use packaging). Pin the pattern to the fabric, and using the tracer, transfer the pattern firmly to the fabric.

3

Once the pattern has been transferred, it's a good idea to check it against the original. Use a Chaco pen to add in details or things that didn't get transferred.

Stretching Fabric on a Frame

1

Assemble a rectangular frame, cover it with fabric, and fasten the fabric to the frame with thumbtacks.

2

When stretching the fabric, it's best to fasten it in the center first, then the edges, and finally, in between.

3

Now it's stretched. (If the fabric is smaller than the frame, use thread to sew the edge of the fabric to the frame.)

Using a Hoop

1

Loosen the screw on the outer hoop and separate the pieces. Place the fabric over the inner hoop, and fit the outer hoop over it.

2

Stretch the fabric firmly and tighten the screw.

3

Pull the edges of the fabric to correct any warping or tension in the fabric grain.

How to Use DMC Embroidery Floss No. 25

1

Gently pull the end of one of the six-stranded threads out of its bundle.

2

Cut a section about 19⅝" to 23⅝" long. I find it's easy to work with a length that is a little more than shoulder width.

3

Pull out the number of necessary strands, one by one. Even when working with multiple strands, make sure to pull them out separately and then reassemble them.

4

Putting the necessary strands together, thread them through the appropriately sized needle. If the needle and thread aren't the right size for each other, the needle will create holes in the fabric, or the thread will become unnecessarily chafed and damaged, which makes it difficult to embroider.

How to Make Appliqués

1 Attach double-sided fusible interfacing (with paper backing) to the reverse side of appliqué fabric; then, transfer the pattern to it in reverse.

2 Cut with the paper backing still attached; then, peel it off.

3 Iron the appliqué to the fabric.

How to Use Tulle

Rather than use a pattern for tulle, I cut several egg-shaped pieces and layer them to add nuance. Hold them in place with marking pins; then, secure them with either invisible thread or thread that is the same color as the fabric.

Free-Motion Embroidery

1 Using the free-motion function on a sewing machine, stitch in random directions to layer and attach another fabric. I love this technique because it adds dimension to the fabric.

2 You can also use free-motion stitching for appliqués. (In this photo, I'm using the reverse side of fabric with text printed on it.)

Needle Felting

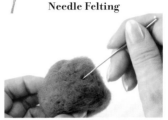

Working with a ball of wool and a specialized needle (the tip is barbed), create whatever shape imaginable simply by stabbing the wool repeatedly into the fabric until it takes the desired form. Be careful not to stab your fingers, though!

Painting

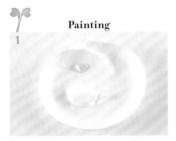

1 In a small dish, squeeze out a small amount of white acrylic paint, along with an even tinier amount of beige acrylic paint.

2 Add water to the white paint and mix in a little beige paint at a time until it reaches the desired consistency. It's okay not to mix the colors completely, leaving the paint with an uneven appearance.

3 Paint the fabric. Rather than painting uniformly, leaving it rough adds a nice touch.

4 Paint lightly where the embroidery will be and heavier where there won't be any stitches. The fabric will lie flat when the paint dries, so don't be afraid to go bold.

Secret Finishing Techniques

1 For a framed project, I finish it by misting the entire work with water while it's still stretched on the frame. (If using this finishing method, it's okay not to iron your project.) I use a Kuramata sprayer, which I recommend because it distributes a fine and even mist.

2 While the work is still damp, moisten the tip of a cotton swab and gently fix the stitches by smoothing them down—you won't believe how much better they will look. This will neaten everything up—satin stitches, outline stitches, everything. (Be careful not to rub too hard, or the thread will become fluffy!)

3 If any pattern marks remain on the fabric, use the tip of a moistened cotton swab to buff them away.

51

French Knot

This is a basic stitch; however, it can be unexpectedly difficult. The biggest challenge may be properly pulling the thread tight with your left hand.

1 Bring the thread through to the front, and wrap the thread around the needle. Wrap twice if you want a double wrap.

2 Insert the needle back through the fabric, 1 to 2 threads over from where you pulled it up.

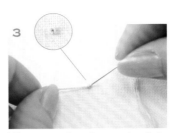

3 With the needle still inserted, pull the thread with your left hand and push the needle through to the reverse side. If you're not careful at this point, the thread will create a bobble instead of a knot.

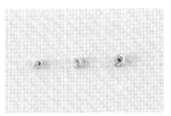

The size of the French knot depends on the number of times you wrap the thread around the needle: 1 wrap, 2 wraps, or 3 wraps. The more wraps you add, the bigger the knot will be.

Weaving Stitch

By passing the thread over or under vertically sewn stiches as if weaving a textile, you can create three-dimensional spindle-shaped parts. This stitch is also known as the raised leaf stitch.

1 Pass the thread from the bottom to the top; then, pull the thread through two more times, just to the right and left sides of the bottom stitch, each time pulling it through the same point at the top.

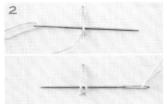

2 Pull the thread back up next to the vertically sewn threads, and pass the needle under the center thread. Then in the opposite direction, pass the needle under the left and right vertical threads.

3 Repeat step 2, alternating the needle under the side of and over the left and right vertical threads (without piercing the fabric). Using the tip of the needle, squeeze the horizontal threads together, spreading out the vertical threads to create a spindle shape.

4 Continue to repeat the steps, keeping the finished shape in mind and adjusting the threads accordingly. When you are done, push the needle through the center stitch at the top.

Ribbon Embroidery

Using embroidery ribbon, it's easy to create a stitch where the thread appears to be hidden.

1 Cut about a 23⅝" length of ribbon, and thread it through the needle. Pierce the end of the ribbon, and pull it through to the other end of the ribbon. This stitch secures the end of the ribbon so it won't come loose while you embroider.

2 Tie a knot at the end of the ribbon, and pull the ribbon through the fabric from the reverse side. Using a single strand of DMC No. 25 in the same color, pull the floss through the fabric next to where the ribbon comes out. Make a running stitch along 19⅝" of the center of the ribbon. (It's okay if the running stitches are not even.)

3 Pull the thread on the running stitches, shortening the 19⅝" length of ribbon to about 2¾".

4 Coil the ribbon around in a circle, and pin it in place. Adjust the gathers as you wrap a second coil, pulling the ribbon through to the reverse side.

5 On the reverse side, finish off the ribbon by sewing it down. Pull the embroidery floss through to the reverse side as well.

6 Bring the embroidery floss back to the front to sew down the edges of the ribbon. While removing the pins, it's a good idea to sew down a few places in the center as well.

7 Finish around the outside with couching. Use a six-stranded length of DMC No. 25, sew the ribbon down with a single strand. I used a contrasting color here to make it easy to see.

8 Sew the ribbon down while coiling the floss around the ribbon.

Straight Stitch

Running Stitch

Repeat 2–3

Outline Stitch

Repeat 2–3

If you overlap too many stitches, the outline will thicken.

Outline as Filling

Fill in the area with outline stitches.

Back Stitch

Couching

Secure with separate thread.

French Knot

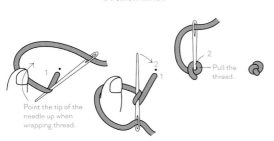

Point the tip of the needle up when wrapping thread.

Pull the thread.

2 Wraps

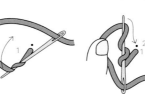

Pull the thread.

French Knot Filling

Fill in the area with French knot stitches.

Open Buttonhole Stitch

Go in either direction.

Buttonhole Stitch

Work open buttonhole stitches close together.

Satin Stitch

When the shape to fill is large, it's best to start in the middle and stitch half at a time.

Padded/Raised Satin Stitch

First sew stitches underneath to add depth.

Long and Short Stitch

Work alternating long and short stitches.

Chain Stitch

Repeat 2–3

Lazy Daisy Stitch

Split Stitch

Work the same as the outline stitch, but split the thread in the middle.

Repeat 2–3

Closing stitch

Fly Stitch

Spiderweb Rose Stitch

Pass under.

Pass under. Pass under. Start coil.

Pass under. Pass under.

Coil the thread, alternating over and under the radial stitches.

Weaving Stitch

Alternate over and under the vertical threads from left to right and back.

HOW TO MAKE

Notes on the Projects and Patterns

* Some of the patterns are actual size, and some have been reduced to 80% of their actual size. Please enlarge the reduced patterns by 125% for actual size.
* Stitch names are shortened in the embroidery patterns to just their main name. For example, satin stitch will be referred to simply as "satin," straight stitch by "straight," lazy daisy stitch by "lazy daisy," and so on.
* The number in parentheses after the stitch name is the color code for DMC embroidery floss, unless noted otherwise.
* When DMC embroidery floss is not used, Kazuko Aoki Original linen thread is used. Kazuko Aoki Original linen thread is indicated by "linen (color name)." Please refer to page 94 for the retailer. This thread is not widely available outside of Japan; as a substitution we suggest DMC Linen Embroidery Floss.
* In the embroidery patterns the type of DMC embroidery floss used is indicated by "#."
* When the thread type is not indicated, use DMC No. 25. Please combine and use the specified number of strands.
* When something other than DMC No. 25 is noted, use 1 strand.
* For French knot stitches, the size depends on the number of wraps and the tension in the thread. In this book, use single wraps unless specified otherwise, but please adjust the size of the knots as necessary for balance.
* The fabric to be embroidered is specified in the materials lists as "Fabric," and other fabrics used as materials for the projects are listed under "Other."

 **SPRING FLOWERS**

Materials

* Thread: DMC embroidery floss No. 25 (3688, 155, 157, 368, 320, 989, 3347, 612, 3822, 822); DMC embroidery floss No. 5 (368)
* Fabric: Linen, white, 13" x 7⅞"
* Other: Fusible interfacing, 13" x 7⅞"

Notes

* Size of embroidery: 6½" x 2⅜"
* Apply fusible interfacing to the reverse side of the embroidery fabric before embroidering.
* Use 3 strands, unless noted otherwise.

Embroidery Pattern

(actual size)

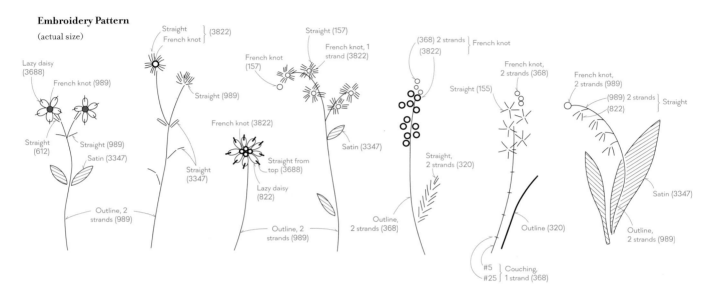

  **SUMMER FLOWERS**

Materials

* Thread: DMC embroidery floss No. 25 (3688, 3607, 156, 3746, 368, 320, 989, 3347, 3822, 801, 822); DMC embroidery floss No. 5 (989)
* Fabric: Linen, white, 13" x 7⅞"
* Other: Fusible interfacing, 13" x 7⅞"

Notes

* Size of embroidery: 6⅝" x 2⅜"
* Apply fusible interfacing to the reverse side of the embroidery fabric before embroidering.
* Use 3 strands, unless noted otherwise.

Embroidery Pattern

(actual size)

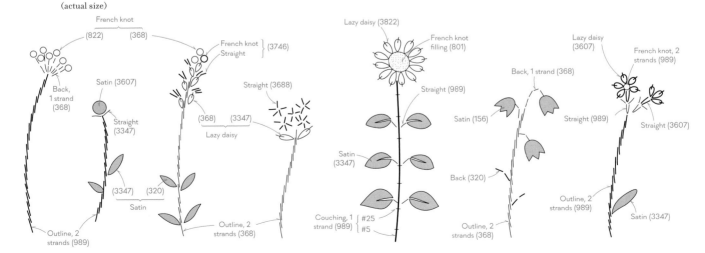

 **AUTUMN FLOWERS**

Materials

* Thread: DMC embroidery floss No. 25 (3712, 327, 155, 931, 368, 320, 989, 3347, 612, 3822, 722, 801, 822, 844); DMC embroidery floss No. 5 (989)
* Fabric: Linen, white, 13" x 7⅞"
* Other: Fusible interfacing, 13" x 7⅞"

Notes

* Size of embroidery: 6⅞" x 2⅛"
* Apply fusible interfacing to the reverse side of the embroidery fabric before embroidering.
* Use 3 strands, unless noted otherwise.

Embroidery Pattern

(actual size)

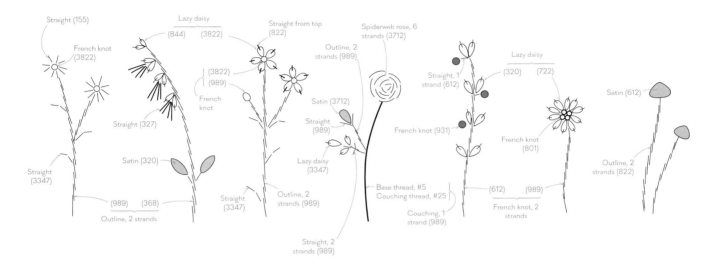

  **WINTER FLOWERS**

Materials

* Thread: DMC embroidery floss No. 25 (3688, 3687, 902, 3325, 368, 320, 989, 3347, 612, 3822, 3776, 822, 844); DMC embroidery floss No. 5 (989); DMC embroidery floss No. 8 (3325)
* Fabric: Linen, white, 13" x 7⅞"
* Other: Fusible interfacing, 13" x 7⅞"

Notes

* Size of embroidery: 6⅞" x 2⅛"
* Apply fusible interfacing to the reverse side of the embroidery fabric before embroidering.
* Use 3 strands, unless noted otherwise.

Embroidery Pattern

(actual size)

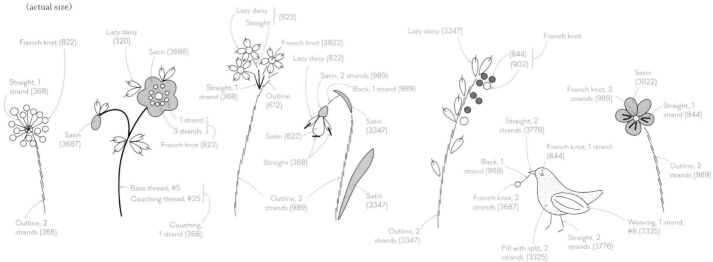

 **SPRING WREATH**

Materials

* Thread: DMC embroidery floss No. 25 (471, 347, 3834, 154, 211, 208, 554, 552, 155, 3746, 333, 823, 3752, 369, 368, 320, 989, 988, 522, 632, 782, 3822, 727, 433, ECRU, 844); DMC embroidery floss No. 5 (471)
* Fabric: Linen, off-white, 13¾" square
* Other: Fusible interfacing, 13¾" square

Notes

* Size of embroidery: 8" x 7⅝"
* Apply fusible interfacing to the reverse side of the embroidery fabric before embroidering.
* Use 3 strands, unless noted otherwise.

Embroidery Pattern

(enlarge by 125%)

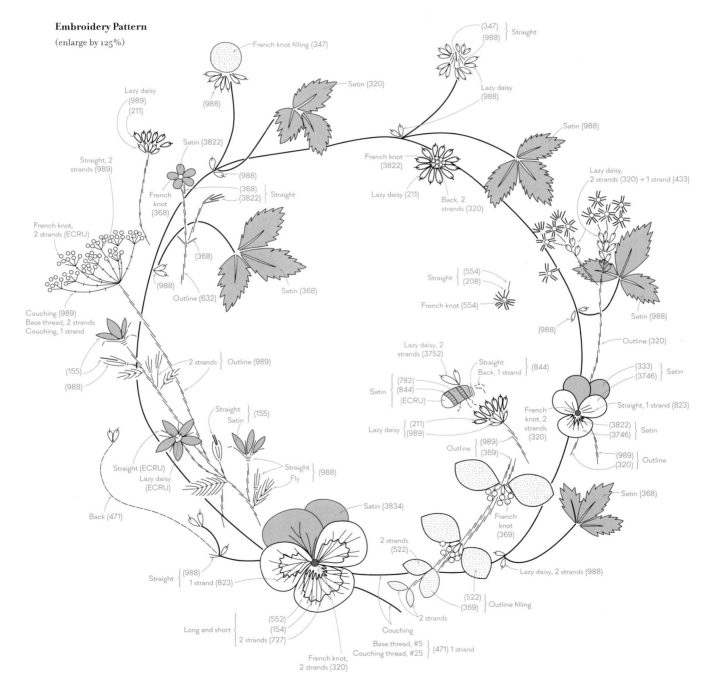

Materials

* Thread: DMC embroidery floss No. 25 (3328, 3688, 3687, 3608, 3835, 155, 3746, 3752, 368, 320, 989, 3347, 704, 3052, 165, 612, 728, 729, 3862, 822, 844, 922); DMC embroidery floss No. 5 (368, 3052, 612)
* Fabric: Linen, off-white, 15¾" square
* Other: Fusible interfacing, 15¾" square

Notes

* Size of embroidery: 8¼" x 7½"
* Apply fusible interfacing to the reverse side of the embroidery fabric before embroidering.
* Use 3 strands, unless noted otherwise.

Embroidery Pattern

(enlarge by 125%)

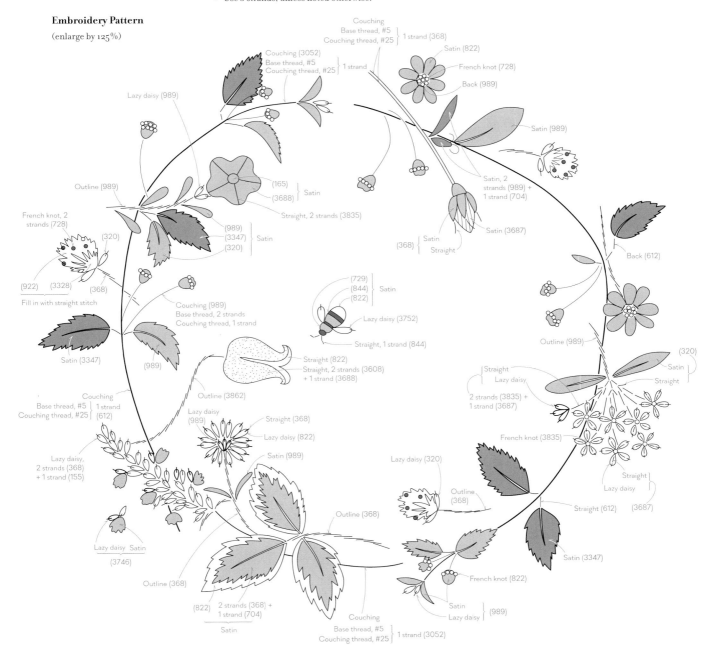

 AUTUMN
WREATH

Materials

* Thread: DMC embroidery floss No. 25 (347, 350, 935, 3053, 524, 3363, 3362, 844); DMC
  embroidery floss No. 5 (524)
* Fabric: Linen, blue-gray, 15" x 15⅜"
* Other: Fusible interfacing, 11" x 15⅜"

Notes

* Size of embroidery: 8¼" x 7⅞"
* Apply fusible interfacing to the reverse side of the embroidery fabric before embroidering.
* Use 3 strands, unless noted otherwise.

Embroidery Pattern

(enlarge by 125%)

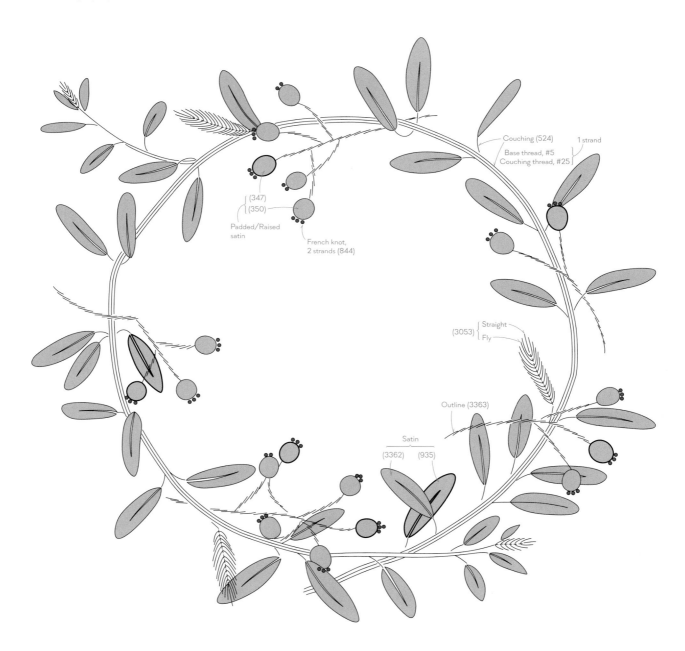

Materials

* Thread: DMC embroidery floss No. 25 (902, 502, 368, 367, 369, 3346, 907, 611, 746, 844);
  DMC embroidery floss No. 5 (369, 611)
* Fabric: Linen, beige, 14½" x 13¾"
* Other: Fusible interfacing, 14½" x 13¾"

Notes

* Size of embroidery: 7⅝" x 7⅞"
* Apply fusible interfacing to the reverse side of the embroidery fabric before embroidering.
* Use 3 strands, unless noted otherwise.

Embroidery Pattern

(enlarge by 125%)

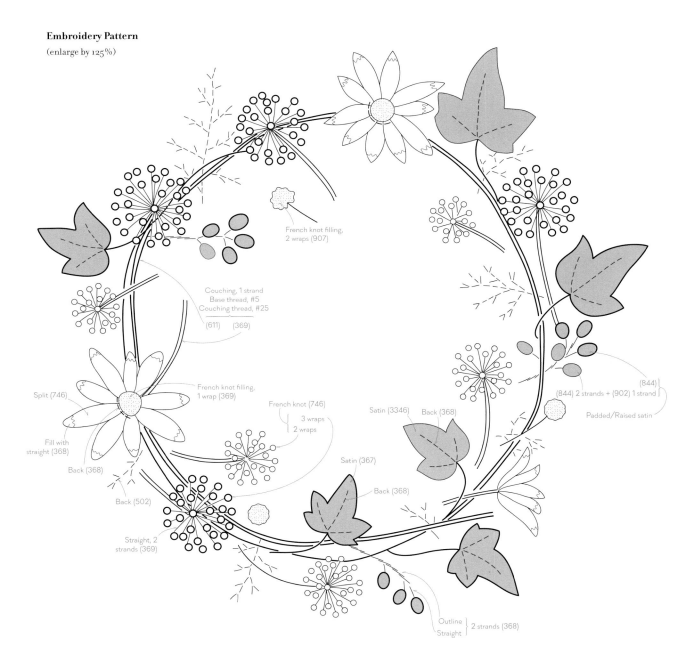

 **TINY DAISIES**

Materials

* Thread: DMC embroidery floss No. 25 (761, 3346, 471, 3362, 3820, 712)
* Fabric: Cotton, light blue with white pin dot, 2¾" wide, length as needed
* Other: Fusible interfacing, same size as fabric

Notes

* Finished size: 2" wide
* Apply fusible interfacing to the reverse side of the embroidery fabric before embroidering.
* Finish the edges with a scalloped machine stitch; then, cut off any excess material.
* Use 3 strands, unless noted otherwise.

Embroidery Pattern

(actual size)

GARDEN DIARY

Materials

* Thread: DMC embroidery floss No. 25 (761, 347, 3836, 3346, 471, 937, 3364, 3363, 3828, 3820, 3852, 712, 3862, 640, 646, 844)
* Fabric: Linen, beige, 19⅝" x 9⅞" (or as needed to fit the journal you are using)
* Other: Fusible interfacing, same size as the fabric

Notes

* Finished size: 6⅛" x 8⅝" x 1⅛" depth
* Apply fusible interfacing to the reverse side of the embroidery fabric before embroidering.
* Fold the flaps, wrong sides together, and sew the top and bottom. Turn the piece right side out, and press it flat.
* Use 3 strands, unless noted otherwise.

How to Cut

Apply fusible interfacing to the reverse side of the embroidery fabric, and finish with zigzag machine stitch

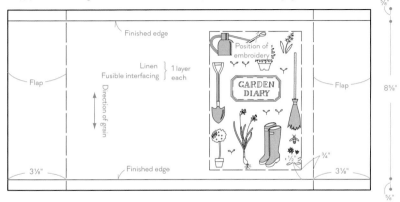

How to Finish

(1) Embroider on the right side

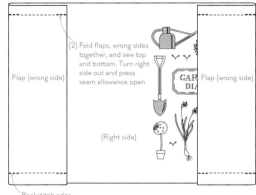

Embroidery Pattern

(actual size)

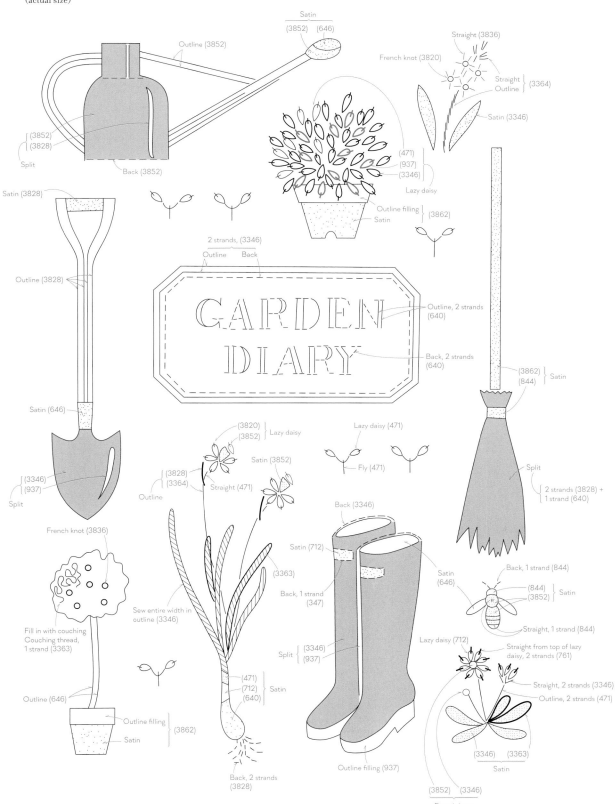

Satin
(3852) (646)

Outline (3852)

Straight (3836)

French knot (3820)

Straight
Outline } (3364)

Satin (3346)

(3852)
(3828) }

Split

Back (3852)

(471)
(937)
(3346) }

Lazy daisy

Outline filling
Satin } (3862)

Satin (3828)

Outline (3828)

2 strands, (3346)
Outline   Back

GARDEN
DIARY

Outline, 2 strands
(640)

Back, 2 strands
(640)

(3862)
(844) } Satin

Satin (646)

(3346)
(937) }

Split

French knot (3836)

(3820)
(3852) } Lazy daisy

Lazy daisy (471)

Satin (3852)

Split

2 strands (3828) +
1 strand (640)

(3828)
(3364) } Outline

Straight (471)

Fly (471)

Back (3346)

Satin (712)

Back, 1 strand (844)

Satin
(646)

(844)
(3852) } Satin

Straight, 1 strand (844)

Fill in with couching
Couching thread,
1 strand (3363)

Sew entire width in
outline (3346)

(3363)

Back, 1 strand
(347)

Lazy daisy (712)

Straight from top of lazy
daisy, 2 strands (761)

Straight, 2 strands (3346)

Outline, 2 strands (471)

Outline (646)

Split
(3346)
(937) }

(471)
(712)
(640) } Satin

Outline filling
Satin } (3862)

Outline filling (937)

Back, 2 strands
(3828)

(3346) (3363)
Satin

(3852)   (3346)
French knot

 COLORS
OF SPRING

Materials

* Thread: Kazuko Aoki Original linen thread (lime green, stem green, leaf green, dark green, primrose, buttercup, strawberry, rose, artichoke, campanula, flax, charcoal); DMC embroidery floss No. 25 (646)
* Fabric: Linen, white, 15³⁄₈" x 14¹⁄₈"
* Other: Fusible interfacing, 15³⁄₈" x 14¹⁄₈"

Notes

* Apply fusible interfacing to the reverse side of the embroidery fabric before embroidering; then, cut the fabric to the desired size.
* Use 1 strand, unless noted otherwise.
* Use linen thread, unless noted otherwise. "#25" denotes No. 25 embroidery floss.

Embroidery Pattern

(actual size)

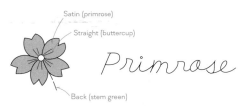

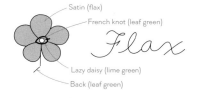

  MINIATURE
GARDEN
SKETCH

Materials

* Thread: DMC embroidery floss No. 25 (3354, 368, 3347, 988, 703, 729, 3863, 822, 648, 844); DMC embroidery floss No. 5 (368, 3347); Kazuko Aoki Original linen thread (lime green, stem green, leaf green, buttercup, rose, artichoke, campanula, flax)
* Fabric: Linen, white, 13³⁄₄" x 16¹⁄₈"
* Other: Fusible interfacing, 13³⁄₄" x 16¹⁄₈"; tulle, 3¹⁄₄" x 3"

Notes

* Size of embroidery: 7⁵⁄₈" x 8⁷⁄₈"
* Apply fusible interfacing to the reverse side of the embroidery fabric before embroidering.
* Use No. 25 embroidery floss unless noted otherwise. "#5" denotes No. 5 embroidery floss, and "linen" denotes Kazuko Aoki thread.
* For No. 25, use 3 strands; for No. 5 and linen, use 1 strand, unless noted otherwise.

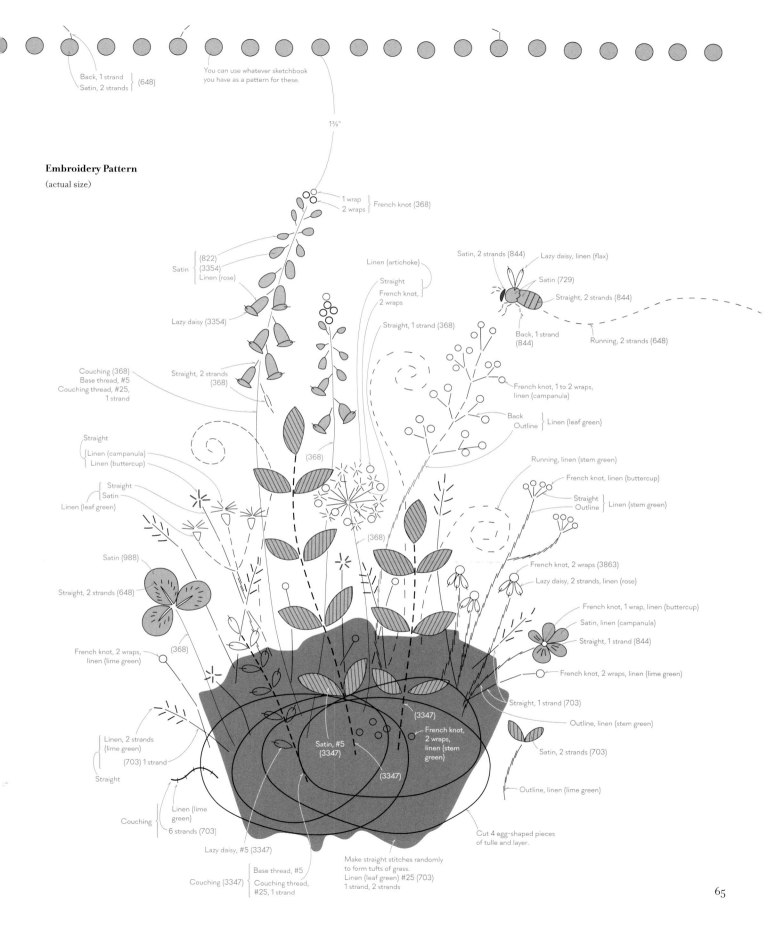

Back, 1 strand
Satin, 2 strands } (648)

You can use whatever sketchbook you have as a pattern for these.

1⅜"

Embroidery Pattern

(actual size)

1 wrap
2 wraps } French knot (368)

Satin { (822)
(3354)
Linen (rose)

Lazy daisy (3354)

Linen (artichoke)

Straight
French knot,
2 wraps

Straight, 1 strand (368)

Satin, 2 strands (844)

Lazy daisy, linen (flax)

Satin (729)

Straight, 2 strands (844)

Back, 1 strand
(844)

Running, 2 strands (648)

Couching (368)
Base thread, #5
Couching thread, #25,
1 strand

Straight, 2 strands
(368)

French knot, 1 to 2 wraps,
linen (campanula)

Back
Outline } Linen (leaf green)

Straight
Linen (campanula)
Linen (buttercup)

(368)

Running, linen (stem green)

French knot, linen (buttercup)

Straight
Outline } Linen (stem green)

Straight
Satin
Linen (leaf green)

(368)

Satin (988)

Straight, 2 strands (648)

French knot, 2 wraps (3863)

Lazy daisy, 2 strands, linen (rose)

French knot, 1 wrap, linen (buttercup)

Satin, linen (campanula)

Straight, 1 strand (844)

French knot, 2 wraps,
linen (lime green)

(368)

French knot, 2 wraps, linen (lime green)

Straight, 1 strand (703)

Outline, linen (stem green)

(3347)

French knot,
2 wraps,
linen (stem
green)

Satin, 2 strands (703)

Linen, 2 strands
(lime green)

(703) 1 strand

Straight

Satin, #5
(3347)

(3347)

Outline, linen (lime green)

Couching

Linen (lime
green)

6 strands (703)

Lazy daisy, #5 (3347)

Couching (3347) {
Base thread, #5
Couching thread,
#25, 1 strand

Make straight stitches randomly
to form tufts of grass.
Linen (leaf green) #25 (703)
1 strand, 2 strands

Cut 4 egg-shaped pieces
of tulle and layer.

Materials

* Thread: DMC embroidery floss No. 25 [Right] (347, 902, 312, 368, 320, ECRU) [Left] (3712, 347, 368, 320)
* Fabric: Linen, light beige with red plaid, 7⅞" square

Notes

* Finished size: 6⅛" diameter (including picot edge)
* Align the center of the fabric with the center of the pattern before embroidering.
* Use 3 strands, unless noted otherwise.
* Stitch the buttonhole picot along a scalloped edge; then, trim excess fabric around the stitched scallop. Be careful not to cut the embroidered thread.
* For the picot at the center of the scalloped edge, make 3 chain stitches to extend past the fabric.

Embroidery Pattern

(actual size)

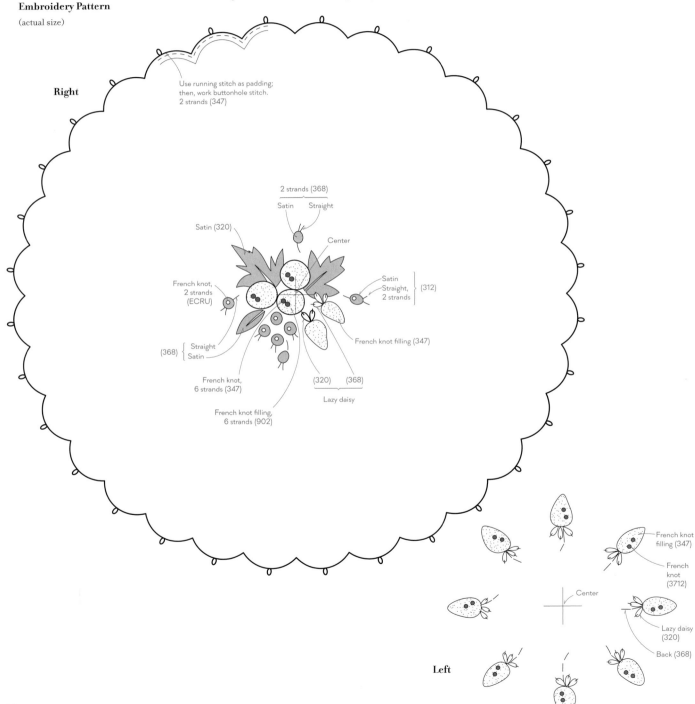

 **JAM JAR BAG**

Materials

* Thread: DMC embroidery floss No. 25 (347)
* Fabric: Linen, beige, 12¼" x 8⅞"
* Other: Plaid linen fabric (used as drawstring), ¼" wide x 20½"; 1 charm

Notes

* Finished size: 5½" x 6⅝"
* Finish the edges of the fabric with a zigzag machine stitch before embroidering the front side.
* With wrong sides together, fold the fabric in half and finish the project as shown in the diagram. Pass the drawstring through and attach the charm.
* Use 3 strands.

How to Cut

Finish edges of the fabric with zigzag machine stitch

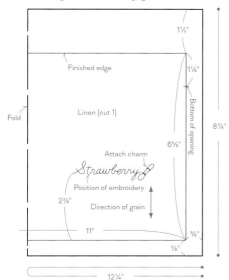

How to Finish

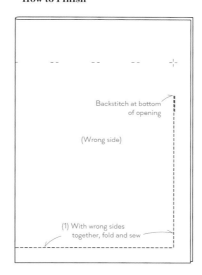

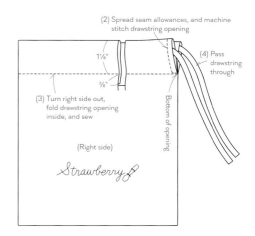

Embroidery Pattern

(actual size)

Outline ⎫
Back ⎭ (347)

Strawberry *Blackberry* *Plum*

Raspberry *Apricot*

❀ POT HOLDER

Materials

* Thread: DMC embroidery floss No. 25 (3712, 347, 902, 312, 368, 320, 3045, ECRU)
* Fabric: Linen, light beige with red plaid, 8¼" square
* Other: Linen, beige, 17¾" x 9"; quilt batting, 8¼" x 9"

Notes

* Finished size: 7" x 7⅞"
* Embroider the pattern. Then stitch the buttonhole picot along a scalloped edge and trim any excess fabric. Layer the embroidered fabric, the beige linen, and the quilt batting, inserting the hanging loop in between, and finish the project as shown in the diagram.
* Use 3 strands, unless noted otherwise.

How to Cut

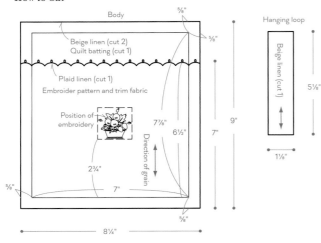

How to Finish

(1) Embroider the pattern

(2) Sew the hanging loop

Fold into quarters and sew both edges

(3) Baste the hanging loop to one piece of beige linen

Beige linen (right side)

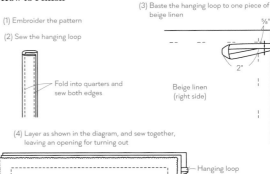

(4) Layer as shown in the diagram, and sew together, leaving an opening for turning out

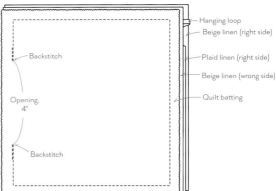

Backstitch
Opening, 4"
Backstitch

Hanging loop
Beige linen (right side)
Plaid linen (right side)
Beige linen (wrong side)
Quilt batting

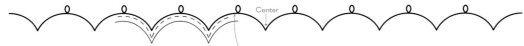

Center

Use running stitch as padding; then, work buttonhole stitch
2 strands (347)
For picot at the center of the scalloped edge, make 3 chain stitches to extend past the fabric

(5) Turn right side out and whipstitch the opening

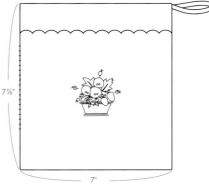

Embroidery Pattern

(actual size)

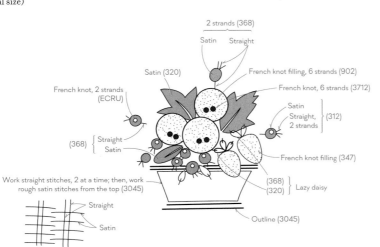

2 strands (368)
Satin   Straight
Satin (320)
French knot, 2 strands (ECRU)
French knot filling, 6 strands (902)
French knot, 6 strands (3712)
Satin
Straight, 2 strands } (312)
(368) { Straight
Satin
French knot filling (347)
Work straight stitches, 2 at a time; then, work rough satin stitches from the top (3045)
(368) } Lazy daisy
(320)
Straight
Satin
Outline (3045)

Materials

* Thread: DMC embroidery floss No. 25 (350, 156, 729, 3822, 3078, 922, 975, 434, 822, 646, 844)
* Fabric: Linen, white, 15⅜" x 12¼"
* Other: Fusible interfacing, 29⅛" x 12¼"; background lining fabric, 13¾" x 11"; quick-drying bond

Notes

* Apply fusible interfacing to the reverse side of the embroidery fabric before embroidering.
* Make a cut around the butterfly wings, lifting them up slightly so that they appear in flight, and use a cotton swab to apply quick-drying bond to the cross section.
* Apply fusible interfacing to the reverse side of the background lining fabric, and layer it under the embroidered fabric.

Embroidery Pattern

(actual size)

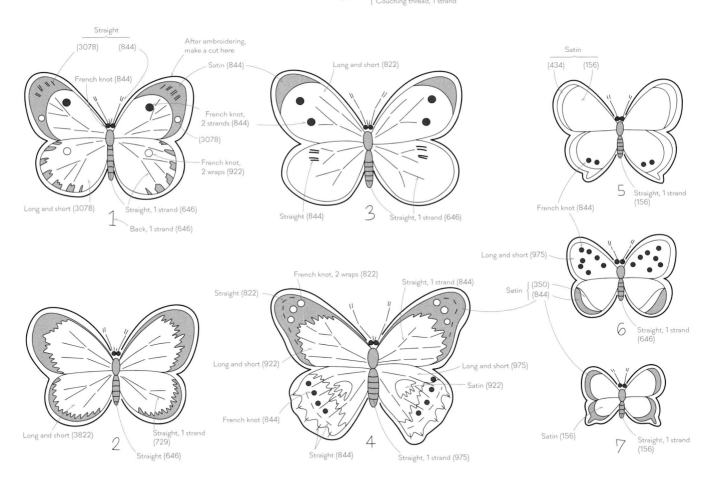

 **BUTTERFLY BROOCH**

Materials

* Thread: DMC embroidery floss No. 25 (822, 646, 844)
* Fabric: Linen, white, 2¾" x 2⅜"
* Other: Fusible interfacing, 2¾" x 2⅜"; backing fabric (choose something that won't fray), 2¾" x 2⅜"; wire, No. 30, No. 32; brooch pin; quick-drying bond

Notes

* Use 3 strands, unless noted otherwise.
* The bodies are all sewn the same way, except for the straight stitches on the belly.
* Use 1 wrap for French knot stitches, unless noted otherwise.

How to Make the Brooch

Apply fusible interfacing to the reverse sides of both the embroidery fabric and the backing fabric

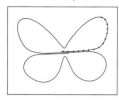

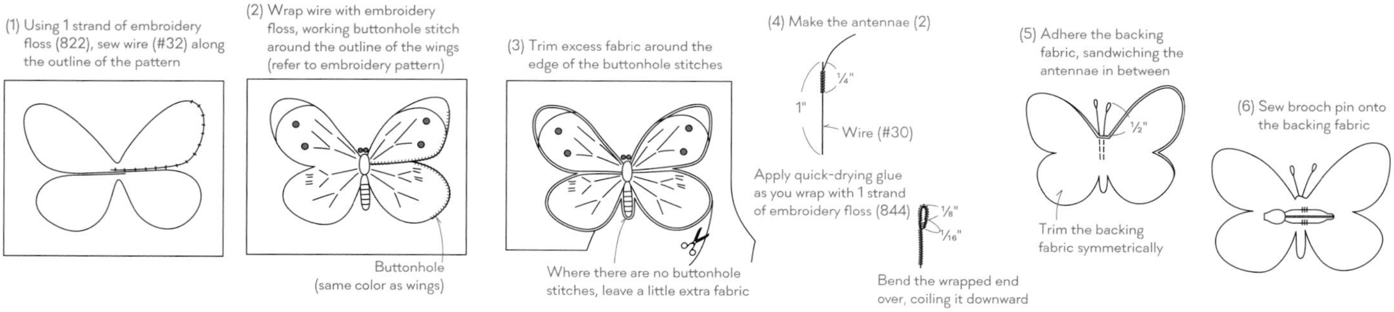

(1) Using 1 strand of embroidery floss (822), sew wire (#32) along the outline of the pattern

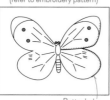

(2) Wrap wire with embroidery floss, working buttonhole stitch around the outline of the wings (refer to embroidery pattern)

Buttonhole (same color as wings)

(3) Trim excess fabric around the edge of the buttonhole stitches

Where there are no buttonhole stitches, leave a little extra fabric

(4) Make the antennae (2)

¼"

1"

Wire (#30)

Apply quick-drying glue as you wrap with 1 strand of embroidery floss (844)

⅛"

1/16"

Bend the wrapped end over, coiling it downward

(5) Adhere the backing fabric, sandwiching the antennae in between

½"

Trim the backing fabric symmetrically

(6) Sew brooch pin onto the backing fabric

  **LAVENDER SACHET**

Materials

* Thread: DMC embroidery floss No. 25 (209, 3746, 368, 320, 383); DMC embroidery floss No. 5 (368)
* Fabric: Linen, beige, 11⅞" x 5½"
* Other: Fusible interfacing, 11⅞" x 5½"; light purple striped cotton fabric, 5½" x 10¼"; alphabet stamps, inkpad for use on fabric (brown); dried lavender, 1½ oz.

Notes

* Finished size: 4¾" square
* Use 3 strands, unless noted otherwise.
* Use No. 25, unless noted otherwise. "#5" denotes No. 5 embroidery floss.

How to Cut

Make ⅜" seam allowances, unless noted otherwise

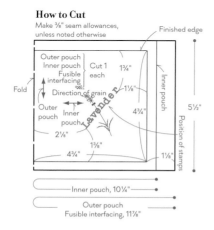

Finished edge

Outer pouch
Inner pouch
Fusible interfacing

Cut 1 each

1¾"

1⅛"

Inner pouch

Direction of grain

Fold

Outer pouch

Inner pouch

4¾"

5½"

Position of stamps

2⅛"

1⅜"

4¾"

1⅛"

Inner pouch, 10¼"

Outer pouch
Fusible interfacing, 11⅞"

Embroidery Pattern

(actual size)

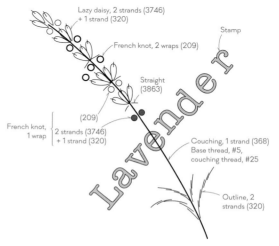

Lazy daisy, 2 strands (3746) + 1 strand (320)

French knot, 2 wraps (209)

Stamp

Straight (3863)

(209)

French knot, 1 wrap

2 strands (3746) + 1 strand (320)

Couching, 1 strand (368)
Base thread, #5, couching thread, #25

Outline, 2 strands (320)

Lavender

How to Finish

(1) Apply fusible interfacing to the wrong side of the outer pouch, and finish with zigzag machine stitch

(2) Stamp lettering on the outer pouch before embroidering

(3) Fold outer pouch fabric in half, with wrong sides together, and sew top and bottom together

(4) Turn right side out, and fold seam allowances of the opening inward

(5) Fold inner pouch fabric in half, wrong sides together, and sew around the edge, leaving opening for turning out

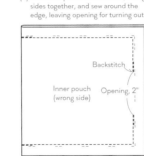

(6) Turn right side out, fill with dried lavender, and whipstitch opening

(7) Insert (6) into outer pouch

---

page 20  **HERB SAMPLER**

Materials

* Thread: DMC embroidery floss No. 25 (3328, 209, 156, 3746, 3752, 368, 320, 989, 3347, 612, 783, 729, 3822, 3821, 3776, 3863, 822, 646, 844); DMC embroidery floss No. 5 (368, 989, 987); DMC embroidery floss No. 8 (712)
* Fabric: Linen: off-white, 19¼" x 14½"; white, 7⅞" x 4"
* Other: Fusible interfacing, 27⅛" x 14½"; ⅛"-wide organdy ribbon, beige, 6¼"; cheesecloth, 7⅞" x 4"; text-print fabric, 3" x 1½"; acrylic paint: white, beige; alphabet stamps; inkpad for use on fabric (brown); quick-drying bond

Notes

* Size of embroidery: 8⅞" x 7½"
* Use 3 strands, unless noted otherwise.
* Use No. 25, unless noted otherwise. "#5" denotes No. 5 embroidery floss.
* Apply fusible interfacing to the reverse side of the embroidery fabric before embroidering.
* First paint the embroidery fabric; then, using the free-motion function, machine stitch the other fabrics to it.
* Using the free-motion function, machine stitch the text-print fabric and cheesecloth onto the off-white linen, allowing the stitches to extend beyond the edge of the fabric. Then, paint the piece with acrylic (refer to page 51).
* Embroider the pattern before stamping the lettering. Embroider the insects on the white linen (patterns below) and cut them out, leaving a little room around the edges. Use quick-drying bond to attach them to the sampler wherever you like.

Embroidery Patterns

(actual size)

* Embroider pattern before cutting out (leave a little fabric around the outside, and apply bond to the cross section using a cotton swab).
* Use 3 strands, unless noted otherwise.
* All French knots are 1 wrap.

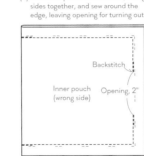

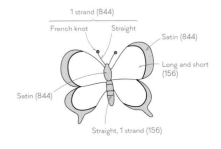

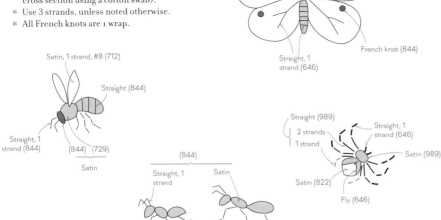

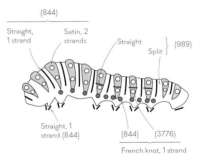

71

Embroidery Pattern

(enlarge by 125%)

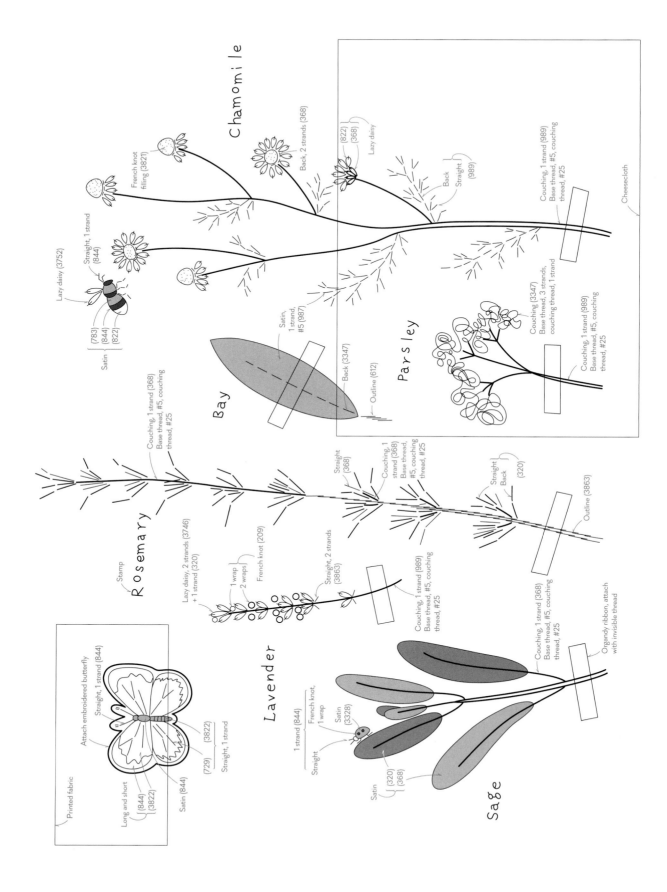

Chamomile

French knot
filing (3821)

Back, 2 strands (368)

(822)
(368)
Lazy daisy

Back

Straight
(989)

Couching, 1 strand (989)
Base thread, #5, couching
thread, #25

Cheesecloth

Straight, 1 strand
(844)

Lazy daisy (3752)

(783)
(844)
(822)

Satin

Satin,
1 strand,
#5 (987)

Back (3347)

Outline (612)

Parsley

Couching (3347)
Base thread, 3 strands,
couching thread, 1 strand

Couching, 1 strand (989)
Base thread, #5, couching
thread, #25

Bay

Rosemary

Stamp

Couching, 1 strand (368)
Base thread, #5, couching
thread, #25

Lazy daisy, 2 strands (3746)
+ 1 strand (320)

1 wrap
2 wraps

French knot (209)

Straight, 2 strands
(3863)

Straight
(368)

Couching, 1
strand (368)
Base thread,
#5, couching
thread, #25

Straight
Back
(320)

Outline (3863)

Couching, 1 strand (989)
Base thread, #5, couching
thread, #25

Printed fabric

Attach embroidered butterfly
Straight, 1 strand (844)

(3822)

(729)   (3822)

Straight, 1 strand

Long and short

(844)
(3822)

Satin (844)

Lavender

Couching, 1 strand (368)
Base thread, #5, couching
thread, #25

Organdy ribbon, attach
with invisible thread

1 strand (844)
French knot,
1 wrap
Satin
(3328)

Straight

Satin

(320)
(368)

Sage

72

EMBROIDERED SILHOUETTES

Materials

* Thread: DMC embroidery floss No. 25 (3799)
* Fabric: Linen, beige, 11½" x 15¾" for each silhouette
* Other: Fusible interfacing, 11½" x 15¾" for each silhouette

Notes

* Size of embroidery: Refer to the pattern.
* Apply fusible interfacing to the reverse side of the embroidery fabric before embroidering.
* Use (3799) for all stitches.
* Use 3 strands, unless noted otherwise.
* Work split stitch, unless noted otherwise.

Embroidery Pattern

(actual size)

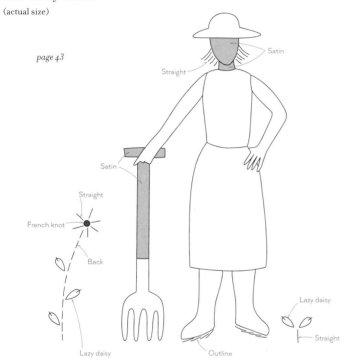

page 43

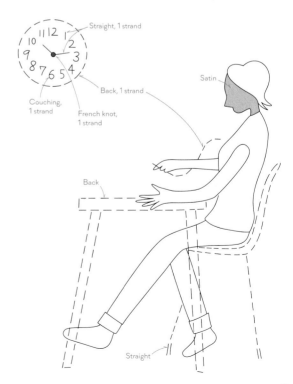

page 48

 **GARDENING SET**

Materials

For the Plastic-Tie Bag
* Thread: DMC embroidery floss No. 25 (520)
* Fabric: 17¾" x 5⅛"
* Other: Fusible interfacing, 1⅜" x ¾"; brown leather, 4" x 1½"; ⅛"-wide brown leather strap, 25½"; 1 charm

For the Hemp Twine Bag
* Thread: DMC embroidery floss No. 25 (520)
* Fabric: Linen blend, beige, 17¾" x 9"
* Other: Fusible interfacing, 4¾" x ¾"; brown leather, 4¾" x 4⅜"; ⅛"-wide brown leather strap, 21⅝"; 1 charm

For the Pruner Cases
* Thread: DMC embroidery floss No. 25 (520)
* Fabric: Thick felt, beige, as needed, for the pruner cases
* Other: Velcro, ½" square; 1 charm

For the Gardening Gloves
* Thread: DMC embroidery floss No. 25 (729, 844) and DMC embroidery floss No. 8 (712)
* Fabric: Gardening gloves (store-bought)

Notes

* Finished sizes: Refer to the diagrams.
* For the gardening gloves, position the embroidery wherever you like. If it's difficult to transfer the pattern, try using piecing paper to transfer the pattern, then iron it on before embroidering.
* Use 3 strands, unless noted otherwise.
* Instructions for embroidering text are the same for all letters.
* "#8" denotes DMC embroidery floss No. 8. Use No. 25, unless noted otherwise.

How to Finish

(1) Apply fusible interfacing to the wrong side of the fabric before embroidering
(2) Sew the leather bottom onto the right side of the bottom of the body

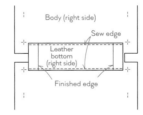

(3) Fold the body in half, right sides together, and sew both sides up to the opening

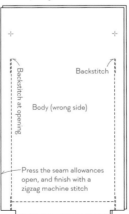

(5) Sew the opening

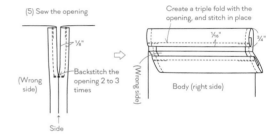

(6) Pass the leather strap through from both sides

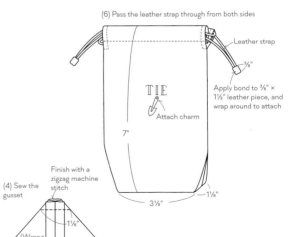

Plastic-Tie Bag

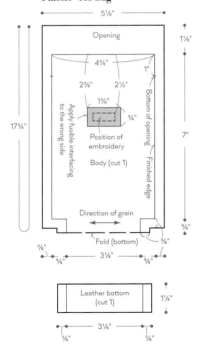

Hemp Twine Bag

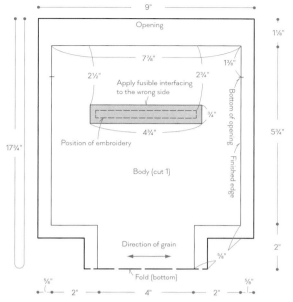

9"

Opening

1⅛"

7⅞"

1⅜"

2½"   2¾"

Apply fusible interfacing
to the wrong side

¾"

4¾"

Position of embroidery

Body (cut 1)

Bottom of opening   Finished edge

5¾"

17¾"

Direction of grain

⅝"

2"

Fold (bottom)

⅝"   2"   4"   2"   ⅝"

Leather bottom
(cut 1)

4"

4"

⅜"   ⅜"

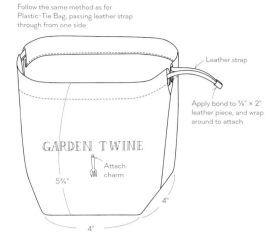

Follow the same method as for
Plastic-Tie Bag, passing leather strap
through from one side

Leather strap

Apply bond to ⅜" × 2"
leather piece, and wrap
around to attach

GARDEN TWINE

Attach
charm

5¾"

4"

4"

How to Finish the Pruner Cases

(1) Make the pattern to fit the size of the pruners
(2) Cut the felt (cut 2, symmetrical), leaving a ⅜" seam allowance all around
(3) Embroider the pattern
(4) With wrong sides together, sew around the edges, leaving an opening
(5) Cut the seam allowances to ⅛"
(6) Sew a ½" square piece of Velcro inside the opening
(7) Attach the charm

Embroidery Pattern

(actual size)

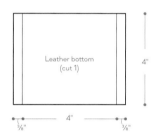

Gardening Gloves

Straight, 1
strand (844)

(844)
(729)   } Satin

Weaving, 1
strand, #8 (712)

Straight (844)

3 strands
2 strands   } Straight
1 strand   (844)

Satin (729)

Plastic-Tie Bag

Outline
Back   } 2 strands (520)

Pruner Case A

Pruner Case B

THE FELCO B & B
2

Hemp Twine Bag

GARDEN TWINE

75

Materials

* Thread: DMC embroidery floss No. 25 (3712, 3328, 3687, 553, 156, 157, 930, 369, 368, 320, 989, 3347, 472, 3053, 3362, 3822, 977, 433, 822); DMC embroidery floss No. 5 (368, 989, 3053)
* Fabric: Linen, off-white, 19" x 15¾"
* Other: Fusible interfacing, 19" x 15¾"; linen, beige, 19" x 4"; linen, blue, 2½" x 3½"; double-sided fusible interfacing, 21⅝" x 4"; tulle, green, 9" x 3⅛"; invisible thread; alphabet stamps; inkpad for use on fabric (dark green); ⅜"-thick Styrofoam board, 15½" x 12⅝"; 48 small nails

Notes

* Finished size: 15½" x 12⅝"
* Apply fusible interfacing to the reverse side of the off-white embroidery fabric, and apply double-sided fusible interfacing to the reverse side of beige (ground) and blue (window) linen before embroidering.
* Attach the beige linen to the off-white linen with a zigzag machine stitch as shown; then, sew it again using the free-motion function. Attach the tulle with invisible thread before embroidering the pattern.
* Stamp the lettering. Then, mount the fabric on the Styrofoam board, securing it with tape on the back before attaching it with 13 nails each to the top and bottom and 11 nails to each side.
* Align the placement marks before transferring the pattern.
* Use 3 strands, unless noted otherwise.
* Use No. 25 embroidery floss, unless noted otherwise. "#5" denotes No. 5 embroidery floss, and "linen" denotes linen thread.
* Use 1 wrap for French knots, unless noted otherwise.

Embroidery Pattern

(actual size)

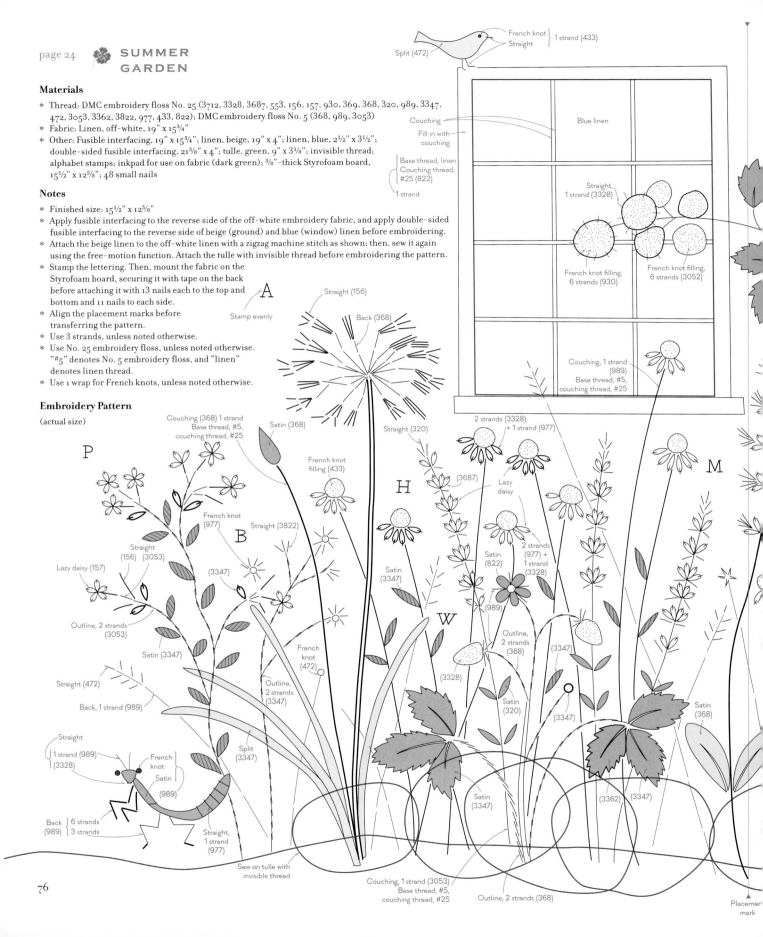

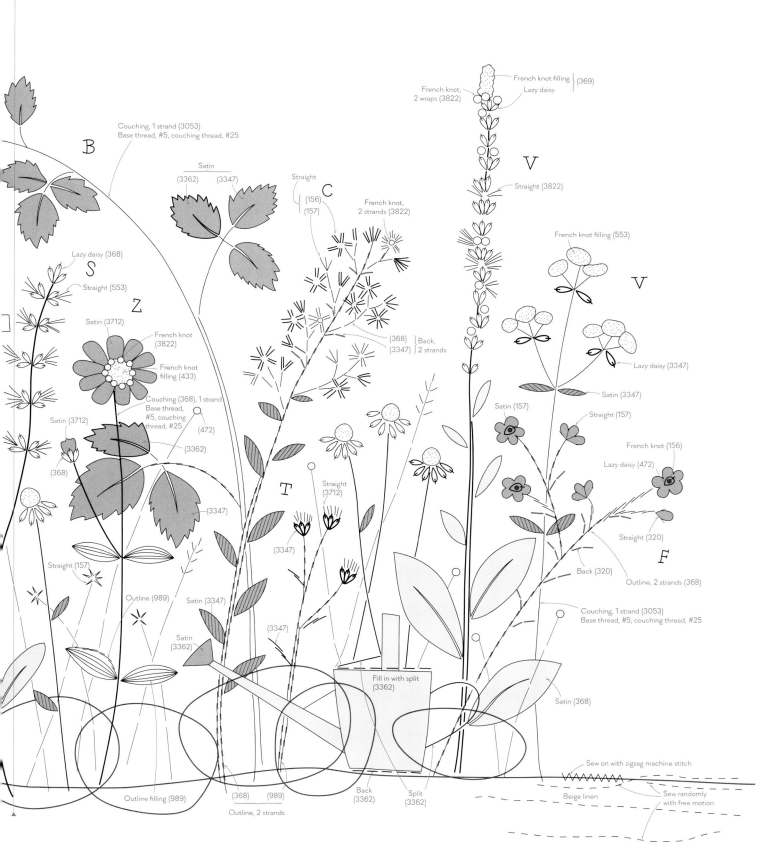

French knot filling
} (369)
Lazy daisy

French knot,
2 wraps (3822)

Couching, 1 strand (3053)
Base thread, #5, couching thread, #25

B

Satin
(3362)   (3347)

Straight

(156)
(157)

C

French knot,
2 strands (3822)

V

Straight (3822)

French knot filling (553)

Lazy daisy (368)

S

Straight (553)

Z

Satin (3712)

French knot
(3822)

French knot
filling (433)

Couching (368), 1 strand
Base thread,
#5, couching
thread, #25

(472)

(3362)

Satin (3712)

(368)

(3347)

(368)
(3347) } Back,
2 strands

V

Lazy daisy (3347)

Satin (3347)

Satin (157)

Straight (157)

French knot (156)

Lazy daisy (472)

T

Straight
(3712)

(3347)

Straight (157)

Outline (989)

Satin (3347)

(3347)

Satin
(3362)

Straight (320)

F

Back (320)

Outline, 2 strands (368)

Couching, 1 strand (3053)
Base thread, #5, couching thread, #25

Fill in with split
(3362)

Satin (368)

Sew on with zigzag machine stitch

Beige linen

Sew randomly
with free motion

Outline filling (989)

(368)   (989)

Outline, 2 strands

Back
(3362)

Split
(3362)

 **POCKET BOARD**

Materials

* Thread: DMC embroidery floss No. 25 (3347, 610, 783, 921, ECRU, 844, 414, 169, 3799, 310)
* Fabric: Linen blend, beige, 31⅞" x 31½"; linen, blue, 7¼" x 8"; linen, mustard, 6⅞" x 8"
* Other: Fusible interfacing, 32⅞" x 31½"; ⅝"-wide grosgrain ribbon, beige, 2½ yards; ⅜"-wide double-sided tape, 22¼"; ¾"-thick corkboard, 17¾" x 23⅝"; staple gun

Notes

* Finished size: 17¾" x 23⅝" x ¾"
* Use 3 strands, unless noted otherwise.

How to Cut

* Use beige linen, unless noted otherwise.
* Cut the fusible interfacing to the same size as the right sides of the body and pockets.
* For the pockets, add the measurements in parentheses for the seam allowances.

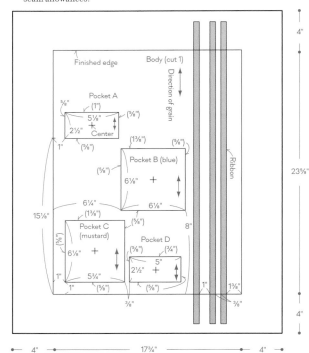

How to Finish

(1) Apply fusible interfacing to reverse sides of the body and pockets, and finish edges with zigzag machine stitch
(2) Align the center of the pocket with the center of the pattern before embroidering
(3) Sew pockets
(4) Wrap body around the corkboard, securing it with a staple gun
(5) Attach the ribbon with a staple gun

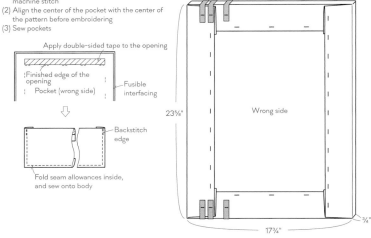

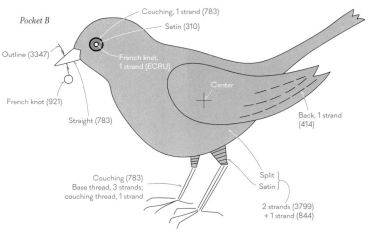

Embroidery Pattern

(actual size)

Pocket A

Couching, 2 strands (844)

 **BIRD COIN PURSE**

Materials

* Thread: DMC embroidery floss No. 25 (610, 921, 3865, 844, 169, 310)
* Fabric: Linen blend, beige, 11⅞" x 5⅛"
* Other: Fusible interfacing, 11⅞" x 5⅛"; lining, quilt batting, 11⅞" x 5⅛" each; 4"-wide clasp; quick-drying bond

Notes

* Finished size: 5½" x 5"
* Apply fusible interfacing to the reverse side of the embroidery fabric before embroidering.
* Finish the project as shown in the diagram and attach a clasp.

How to Finish

(1) Apply fusible interfacing to the reverse side of the outer fabric before embroidering
(2) Layer (1), lining, and quilt batting, and sew each of their wrong sides together

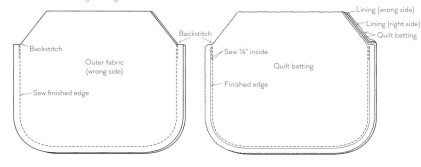

How to Cut

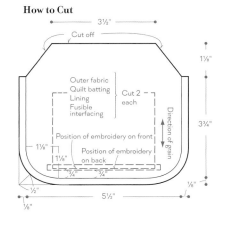

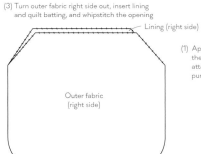

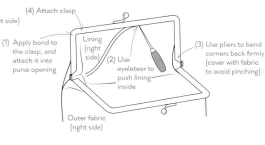

Pocket C, Bird Coin Purse

* For the coin purse, substitute (3865) for (ECRU).

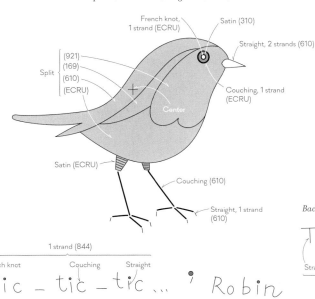

Pocket D   Couching, 1 strand (844)

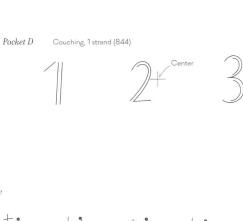

Back of Coin Purse

NEEDLE CASE

Materials

* Thread: DMC embroidery floss No. 25 (729, 645, 844); DMC embroidery floss No. 5 (ECRU)
* Fabric: Linen blend, beige, 6¼" x 8¼"
* Other: Fusible interfacing, 6¼" x 8¼"; cotton fabric for lining, 6¼" x 8¼"; ¼"-wide beige braid, 11¼"; ¹⁄₁₆"-wide leather strap, 10¼"; ½"-wide Velcro, 5⅛"

Notes

* Finished size: Width of opening: 5½"; width of bottom: 4⅜"; depth: 3¾"

How to Make Needle Case

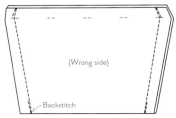

(1) Apply fusible interfacing to reverse side of outer fabric before embroidering front
(2) Fold (1) in half, wrong sides together, and sew sides together

(Wrong side)

Backstitch

(3) Sew lining the same way, wrong sides together

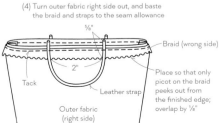

(4) Turn outer fabric right side out, and baste the braid and straps to the seam allowance

⅝"

2"

Tack

Leather strap

Outer fabric (right side)

Braid (wrong side)

Place so that only picot on the braid peeks out from the finished edge; overlap by ⅛"

(5) Fold seam allowance, overlapping lining and Velcro, and sew the opening

Velcro (loop)

Lining (right side)

Braid (right side)

Lining (wrong side)

Velcro (hook) (wrong side)

Needle

Front

Needle Case Pattern and Embroidery Pattern

(actual size)

* Use 3 strands, unless noted otherwise.
* Use No. 25, unless noted otherwise. "#5" denotes No. 5 embroidery floss.

Scissor Keeper/Fob Pattern and Embroidery Pattern

(actual size)

* Use 1 strand. Work as couching (base thread, #8; couching thread, #25; both in ECRU).

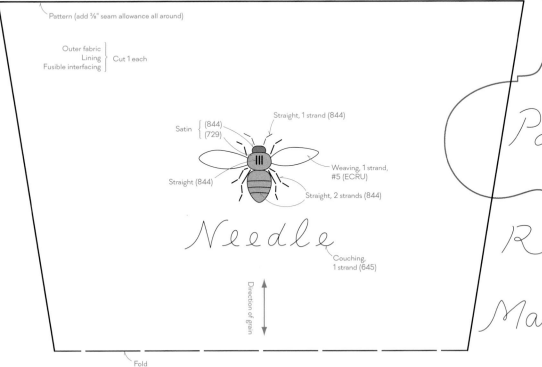

Pattern (add ⅜" seam allowance all around)

Outer fabric
Lining
Fusible interfacing } Cut 1 each

Satin { (844) (729)

Straight, 1 strand (844)

Straight (844)

Weaving, 1 strand, #5 (ECRU)

Straight, 2 strands (844)

Needle

Couching, 1 strand (645)

Direction of grain

Fold

Pattern

Felt (cut 2)

Pansy

Rose

Margaret

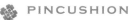

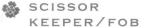

page 30 **PINCUSHION**

Materials

* Thread: DMC embroidery floss No. 25 (729, 844); DMC embroidery floss No. 5 (ECRU)
* Fabric: Linen blend, beige, 6" square
* Other: ¼"-wide beige braid, 7⅞"; wool, as needed; 2"-diameter circle of thick paper or cardboard; flowerpot with an interior diameter of 2⅜"; quick-drying bond

Notes

* Finished size: Refer to diagram.

page 31 **SANDBAG**

Materials

* Thread: DMC embroidery floss No. 25 (729, 844); DMC embroidery floss No. 5 (ECRU)
* Fabric: Linen blend, beige, 8⅝" x 13¾"
* Other: Fusible interfacing, 2" x 1⅛"; cotton fabric for inner bag (use something tightly woven), 8⅝" x 13¾"; ¼"-wide beige braid, 17⅜"; sand, 3¼ lbs

Notes

* Finished size: Refer to diagram.

page 30 **SCISSOR KEEPER/FOB**

Materials

* Thread: DMC embroidery floss No. 25 (ECRU); DMC embroidery floss No. 5 (ECRU)
* Fabric: Felt, blue-gray, mustard, brown, 3" x 3¾" for each item
* Other: 1/16"-wide leather strap, 7⅞" for each item; 1 charm for each item

Notes

* Finished size: Refer to diagram.

How to Cut the Sandbag

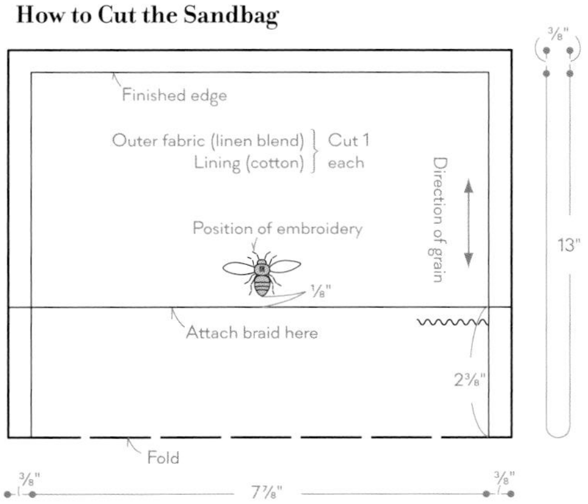

Finished edge
Outer fabric (linen blend) } Cut 1
Lining (cotton) } each
Direction of grain
Position of embroidery
⅛"
Attach braid here
2⅜"
Fold
⅜"
7⅞"
⅜"
⅜"
13"

How to Make the Sandbag

(1) Apply fusible interfacing to the reverse side of embroidery on the outer fabric before embroidering (refer to needle case for pattern)
(2) Sew braid onto the outer fabric
(3) Fold the outer fabric in half, wrong sides together, and sew edges together

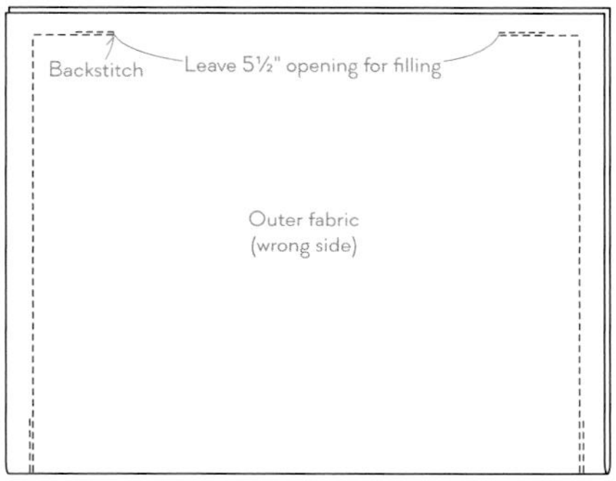

Backstitch
Leave 5½" opening for filling
Outer fabric
(wrong side)

(4) Make the gusset and sew the bottom; then, turn right side out

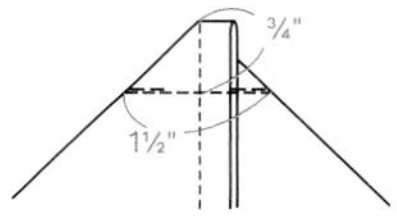

¾"
1½"

(5) Sew the inner bag the same way as for the outer fabric, fill with sand, and whipstitch the opening

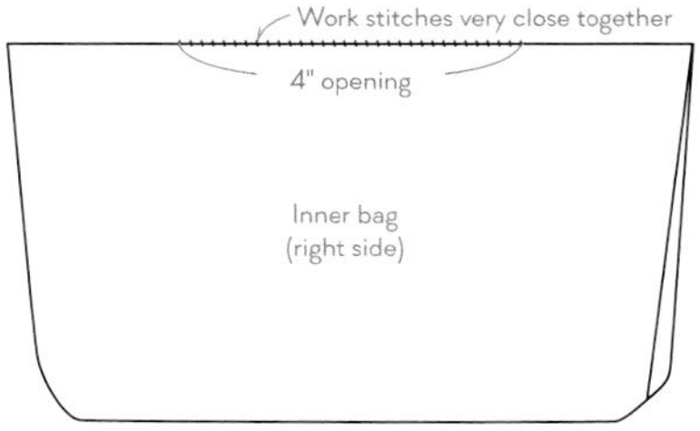

Work stitches very close together
4" opening
Inner bag
(right side)

(6) Insert (5) into outer fabric, and whipstitch the opening

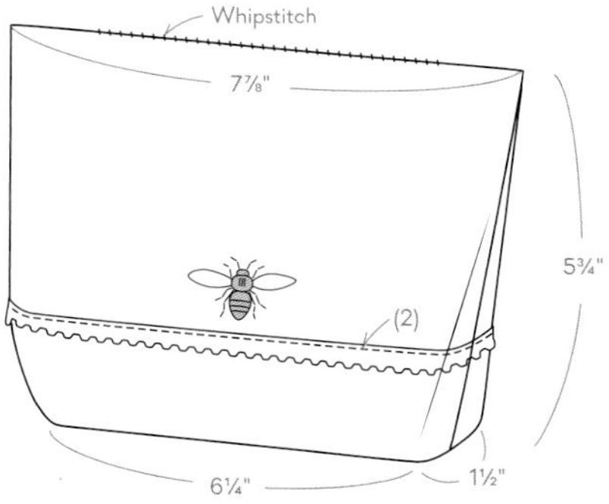

Whipstitch
7⅞"
5¾"
(2)
6¼"
1½"

How to Make Pincushion

(1) Embroider the pattern in the center of 6"-square linen blend (refer to needle case for pattern)
(2) Cut (1) into 4¾"-diameter circle
(3) Place the wool on cardboard or paper, cover with linen, and gather in place using running stitch

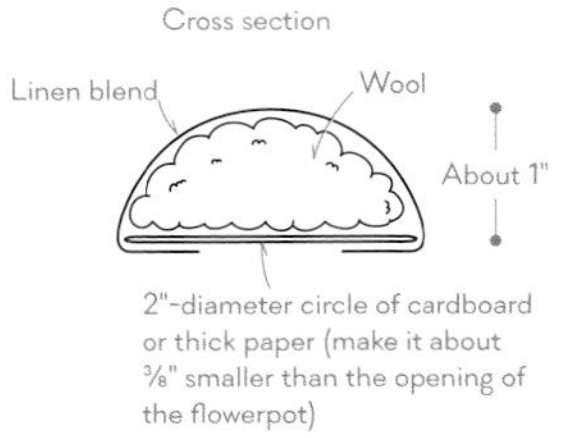

Cross section
Linen blend
Wool
About 1"
2"-diameter circle of cardboard or thick paper (make it about ⅜" smaller than the opening of the flowerpot)

(4) Glue braid to the interior of the flowerpot

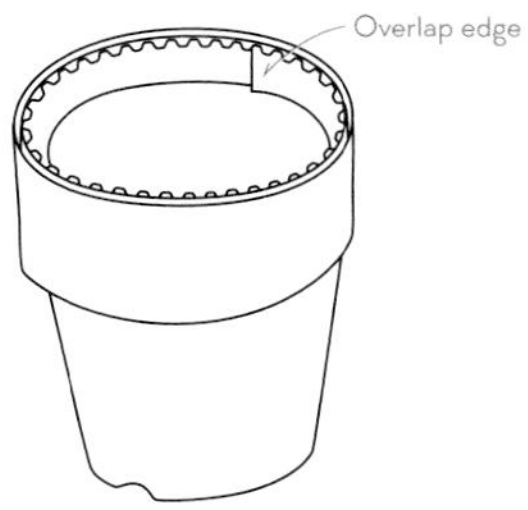

Overlap edge

(5) Insert (3) inside of (4)

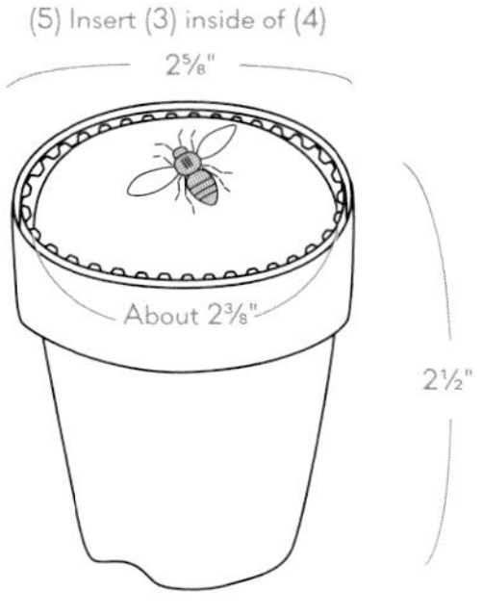

2⅝"
About 2⅜"
2½"

How to Make the Scissor Keeper/Fob

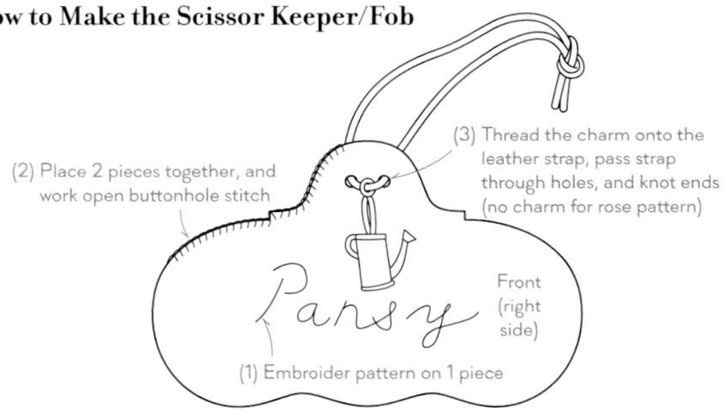

(2) Place 2 pieces together, and work open buttonhole stitch
(3) Thread the charm onto the leather strap, pass strap through holes, and knot ends (no charm for rose pattern)
Pansy
Front
(right side)
(1) Embroider pattern on 1 piece

MUSICAL CLEF TOPIARY

Materials

* Thread: DMC embroidery floss No. 25 (368, 704, 906, 905); DMC embroidery floss No. 5 (612); Kazuko Aoki Original linen thread (primrose)
* Fabric: Linen, off-white, 11" square
* Other: Fusible interfacing, 11" square; linen, beige, 11" x 2¾"; cotton/linen fabric, green, 2⅜" x 4½"; tulle, green, 2⅜" x 4½"; cheesecloth, 4¾" x 2⅛"; text-print fabric, 1⅛" x 4"; double-sided fusible interfacing, 2⅜" x 4½"; wire (annealed), 11⅞"; invisible thread; ⅜"-thick Styrofoam board, 7" square; acrylic paint: white, beige; 28 small nails

Notes

* Finished size: 7" square
* Apply fusible interfacing to the reverse side of the embroidery fabric. Using the free-motion function, machine stitch the beige linen, cheesecloth, and text-print fabric to the off-white linen. Lightly paint the entire piece with acrylic (refer to page 51). Cut the green cotton/linen and tulle into the shape of a musical clef. Then, use the free-motion function to sew the pieces onto the off-white linen again, allowing the machine stitches to extend beyond the edges. Embroider the pattern. Bend the wire into the shape of musical notes, and secure them to the fabric with invisible thread. Mount the fabric on the Styrofoam board, securing it with tape on the back before attaching it with 7 nails along each side.
* Use No. 25, unless noted otherwise. "#5" denotes No. 5 embroidery floss, and "linen" denotes linen thread.
* Machine stitch all fabric using the free-motion function.

Embroidery Pattern

(actual size)

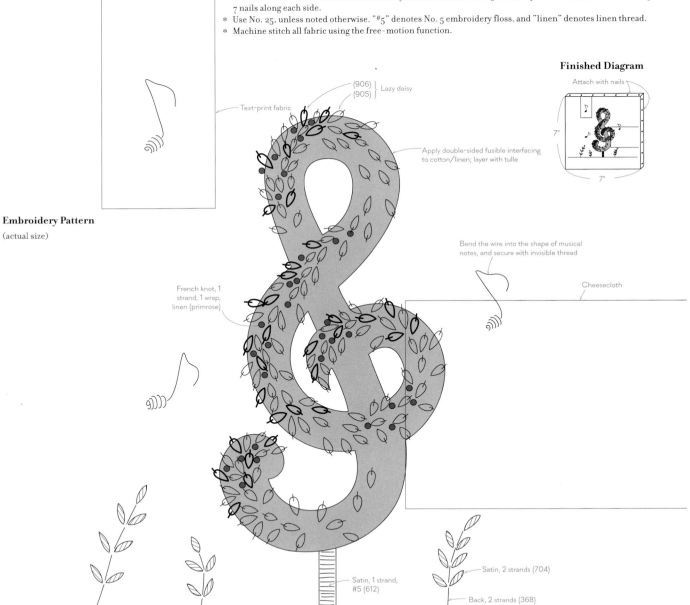

FLORAL DRESS FORM

Materials

* Thread: DMC embroidery floss No. 25 (368, 472, 704, 906, 905)
* Fabric: Linen, off-white, 10⅝" x 13⅜"
* Other: Fusible interfacing, 10⅝" x 13⅜"; text-print fabric, 5⅛" x 1⅜"; cotton/linen fabric, green, 2" x 4"; tulle, green, 2" x 4"; cheesecloth, 2⅜" x 3⅜"; organdy, green, 3½" x 1"; Hobbyra Hobbyre Kazuko Aoki Original embroidery patches in daisy, rose, and zinnia; double-sided fusible interfacing, 2" x 4"; wire (annealed), 11"; lead sheet, 1⅛" square; invisible thread; ⅜"-thick Styrofoam board, 6⅝" x 9½"; acrylic paint in white, beige; 34 small nails

Embroidery Pattern

(actual size)

Text-print fabric

Notes

* Finished size: 6⅝" x 9½"
* Apply fusible interfacing to the reverse side of embroidery fabric before embroidering. Using the free-motion function, machine stitch the cheesecloth and the text-print fabric onto the off-white linen. Lightly paint the entire piece with acrylic (refer to page 51), and attach the organdy with invisible thread. Cut the green cotton/linen and tulle into the shape of a dress form; then, use the free-motion function to sew the piece onto the off-white linen, allowing the machine stitches to extend beyond the edges. Embroider the pattern. Bend the wire into the shape of the dress form stand, and secure it with invisible thread. Cut the lead sheet to size, and attach it with quick-drying bond. Iron on the patches, and mount the fabric on the Styrofoam board, securing it with tape on the back before attaching it with 7 nails each to the top and bottom and 10 nails to each side.
* Work a straight stitch, unless noted otherwise.
* Work straight stitches randomly with 2 or 3 strands, unless noted otherwise.
* Machine stitch all fabric using the free-motion function.

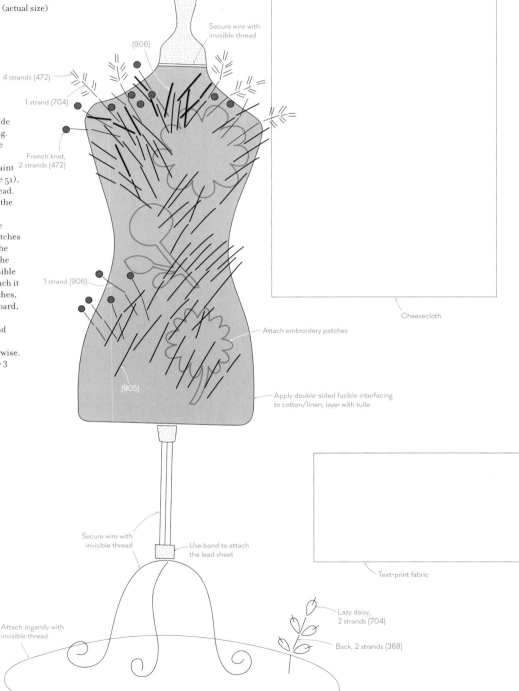

Use bond to attach the lead sheet

Secure wire with invisible thread

(906)

4 strands (472)

1 strand (704)

French knot, 2 strands (472)

Cheesecloth

1 strand (906)

Attach embroidery patches

Apply double-sided fusible interfacing to cotton/linen; layer with tulle

(905)

Secure wire with invisible thread

Use bond to attach the lead sheet

Text-print fabric

Lazy daisy, 2 strands (704)

Back, 2 strands (368)

Attach organdy with invisible thread

 **VASE OF FLOWERS**

Materials

* Thread: DMC embroidery floss No. 25 (3731, 315, 340, 157, 368, 367, 989, 3347, 472, 471, 3828, 3822, 922, 632, 3863); DMC embroidery floss No. 5 (368, 989)
* Fabric: Linen, white, 7⅞" x 9½"
* Other: Fusible interfacing, 7⅞" x 9½"; cheesecloth, 3" x 1⅜"; organdy, light green, 2" x ¾"; text-print fabric, 1½" x ¾"; wire (annealed), 8¼"; invisible thread; ⅜"-thick Styrofoam board, 4¾" x 6¼"; acrylic paint in white, beige; 24 small nails

Notes

* Finished size: 4¾" x 6 ¼"
* Apply fusible interfacing to the reverse side of embroidery fabric before embroidering. Using the free-motion function, machine stitch the cheesecloth and the text-print fabric onto the white linen. Lightly paint the entire piece with acrylic (refer to page 51), and attach the organdy with invisible thread. Embroider the pattern. Bend the wire into the shape of a pitcher, and secure it with invisible thread. Cut the lead sheet to size, and attach it with bond. Mount the fabric on the Styrofoam board, securing it with tape on the back before attaching it with 5 nails each to the top and bottom and 7 nails to each side.
* Use 3 strands, unless noted otherwise.
* Use No. 25 embroidery floss, unless noted otherwise. "#5" denotes No. 5 embroidery floss.
* Machine stitch all fabric using the free-motion function.

Embroidery Pattern

(actual size)

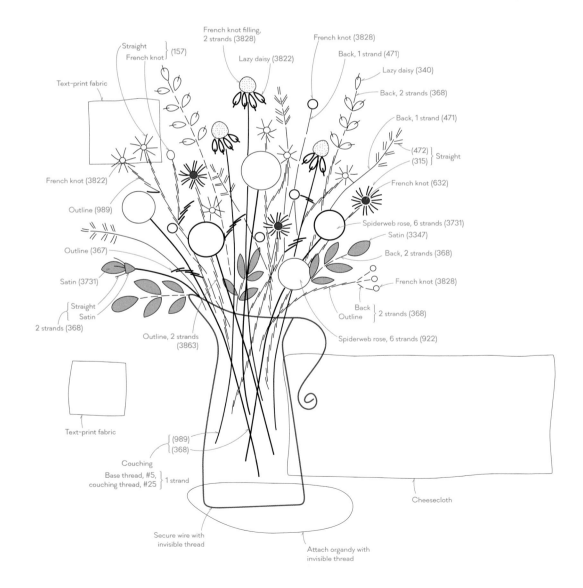

 # BULB PINCUSHION

Materials

* Thread: DMC embroidery floss No. 25 (612); DMC embroidery floss No. 5 (ECRU; not necessary if placing the bulb in a flowerpot)
* Other: Wool, off-white and shades of brown, as needed; $\frac{1}{2}$"-wide satin ribbon, green, $1\frac{1}{2}$" (per bulb); $1\frac{1}{8}$" interior diameter flowerpot; felting needle(s)

How to Make Bulb Pincushion

(1) Form the wool into a largish ball, and use a felting needle to create a bulb shape; embroider the pattern

Bulb

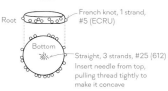

Root

French knot, 1 strand, #5 (ECRU)

Bottom

Straight, 3 strands, #25 (612) Insert needle from top, pulling thread tightly to make it concave

Making a root is not necessary if placing the bulb in a flowerpot

(2) Make the shoot

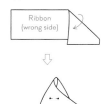

Ribbon (wrong side)

Wrap from the end, and sew down

(3) Attach the shoot

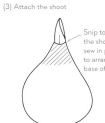

Snip top of the bulb and insert the shoot, adjust shape, and sew in place; use felting needle to arrange wool to hide the base of the shoot

For a large bulb, insert 2 shoots

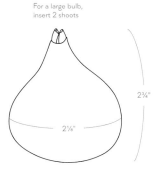

$2\frac{1}{8}$"

$2\frac{3}{4}$"

(4) Attach the root to the bulb

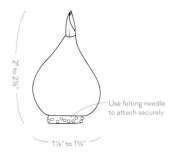

2" to $2\frac{3}{8}$"

Use felting needle to attach securely

$1\frac{1}{8}$" to $1\frac{3}{8}$"

  # BEE PINCUSHION

Materials

* Thread: DMC embroidery floss No. 25 (729, 310); DMC embroidery floss No. 5 (ECRU)
* Other: Wool, green, as needed; 2"-diameter piece of cardboard; $2\frac{1}{2}$" interior diameter flowerpot; felting needle(s)
* Use No. 25, unless noted otherwise

How to Make Bee Pincushion

(1) Form the wool into a ball, and use a felting needle to stab the wool so that it firms up as in the diagram

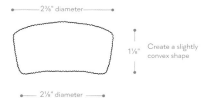

$2\frac{3}{8}$" diameter

$1\frac{1}{8}$"

Create a slightly convex shape

$2\frac{1}{8}$" diameter

Make the diameter slightly smaller than the flowerpot's interior diameter

(2) Embroider pattern on top of (1)

(3) Insert cardboard cut to 2" diameter inside the flowerpot, and insert (2) on top of cardboard

$2\frac{1}{2}$"

About $2\frac{3}{8}$"

3"

Embroidery Pattern

(actual size)

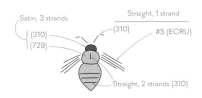

Satin, 3 strands

(310)

(729)

Straight, 1 strand

(310)

#5 (ECRU)

Straight, 2 strands (310)

 **THROW PILLOWS**

Materials

* Thread: DMC embroidery floss No. 25 [Small] (3799) [Medium] (988, 801, 3033) [Large]
  (3347, 987, 347, 704, 470, 976, 433, 3865, 3799)
* Fabric: Linen [Small] ochre, 3½" x 4¾" [Medium] beige and green stripe, 24½" x 12¼"
  [Large] beige, 33⅞" x 17"
* Other: [Small] fusible interfacing, 3½" x 4¾"; linen, green, 20½" x 10¼"; cotton batting,
  3 oz. [Medium] fusible interfacing, 2⅜" x 3⅛"; cotton batting, 3 ½ oz. [Large] fusible
  interfacing, 7⅞" x 3⅛"; pillow insert, 15¾" square

Notes

* Finished size: [Small] 9" square [Medium] 11" square [Large] 15¾" square

How to Cut

Finish the edges of the fabric with zigzag machine stitch

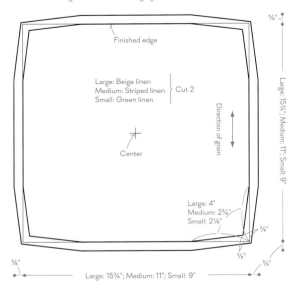

⅝"

Finished edge

Large: Beige linen
Medium: Striped linen   Cut 2
Small: Green linen

Direction of grain

Center

Large: 15¾"; Medium: 11", Small: 9"

Large: 4"
Medium: 2¾"
Small: 2⅛"

⅜"

⅜"

⅝"

⅝"

⅝"

Large: 15¾"; Medium: 11"; Small: 9"

How to Finish

(1) Apply fusible interfacing to the reverse side of the center front
for medium and large size, and to the reverse side of the pocket
for the small size, before embroidering the pattern. For the small
size, fold seam allowances and sew onto the center front

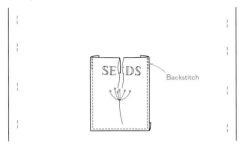

SEEDS

Backstitch

(2) Align front and back, right sides together, and
sew together, leaving an opening for filling

(Wrong side)

Backstitch   Opening   Backstitch

Large: 15¾"; Medium: 5½"; Small: 4¾"

(3) Turn right side out, fill with batting (for the large
size, insert pillow), and whipstitch the opening

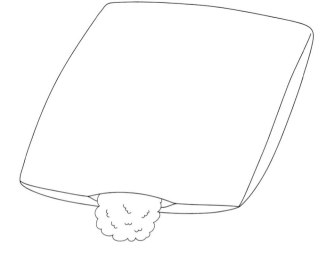

Embroidery Pattern

(actual size)

Small

* Work all stitches with (3799), and use 2 strands, unless noted otherwise.

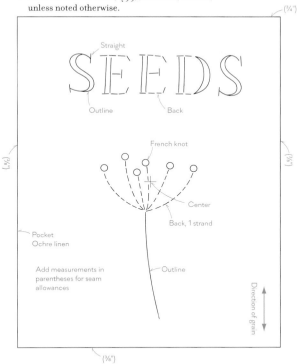

Straight

SEEDS

Outline   Back

French knot

Center

Back, 1 strand

Pocket
Ochre linen

Add measurements in
parentheses for seam
allowances

Outline

(¾")

(⅞")

(⅜")

Direction of grain

Medium

* Use 3 strands, unless noted otherwise.

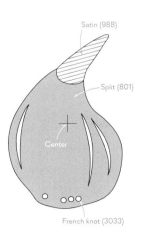

Satin (988)

Split (801)

Center

French knot (3033)

Large

* Use 3 strands, unless noted otherwise.

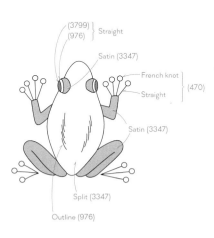

(3799)
(976) } Straight

Satin (3347)

French knot

Straight

(470)

Satin (3347)

Split (3347)

Outline (976)

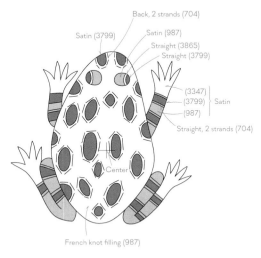

Back, 2 strands (704)

Satin (3799)   Satin (987)

Straight (3865)
Straight (3799)

(3347)
(3799) } Satin
(987)

Straight, 2 strands (704)

Center

French knot filling (987)

How to Embroider the Body

(1) Work spots in satin stitch (3799)
(2) Fill in the rest of the body with French knot filling (987)
(3) Work back stitch using 2 strands (704)

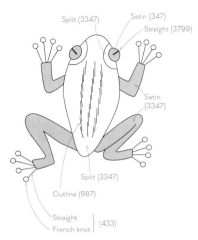

Split (3347)   Satin (347)

Straight (3799)

Satin
(3347)

Split (3347)

Outline (987)

Straight
French knot } (433)

 **CHRISTMAS ORNAMENTS**

Materials

* Thread: DMC embroidery floss Diamant Metallic (D3821)
* Fabric: Wool felt [A] gray, 5¾" x 3⅛" [B] red, 5¾" x 3⅛" [C] gray, 5⅜" x 3½" [D] red, 9½" x 4" [E] red, 4¾" x 4⅛" [Stocking] red, 12¼" x 13⅜"
* Other: Small round beads, gold [A] (6) [B, C, E] as needed; small charm [B]; ⅜"-wide ribbon, gold [A, B, C, E] 1½" each; [D] linen thread; 1½ yards; hemp twine [E] 7⅞" [Stocking] 11⅞"; [E] cotton batting, small amount; quick-drying bond

Notes

* Finished sizes (not including hanging twine): [A, B, C] Refer to pattern [D] 55⅛" long square [E] 2⅛" x 3⅛" [Stocking] 10⅝" x 6⅝"
* For the stocking, embroider the pattern on the front and fold over the cuff, aligning the outer edges of the 2 pieces. Then sew around the edges. Fold the hemp twine in half and knot the ends; then, whipstitch it to the inside of the stocking.

How to Make
A–C

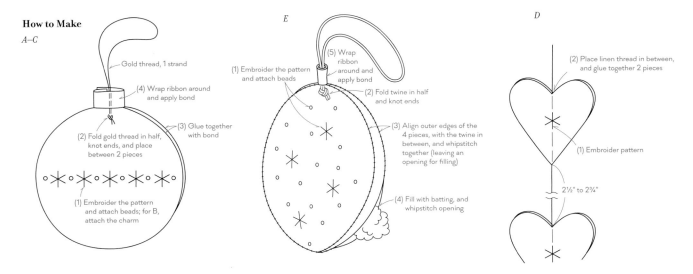

Patterns and Embroidery Patterns

(A–E are actual size; enlarge the stocking by 125%)

* Cut out the felt.
* Work 2 strands of gold thread in straight stitch, unless noted otherwise.
* For B, C, and E, place the beads evenly, wherever you like on the felt.

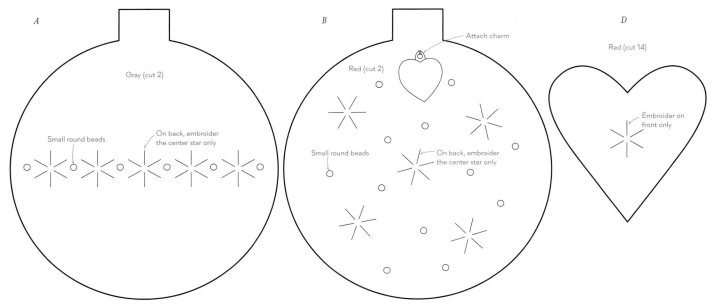

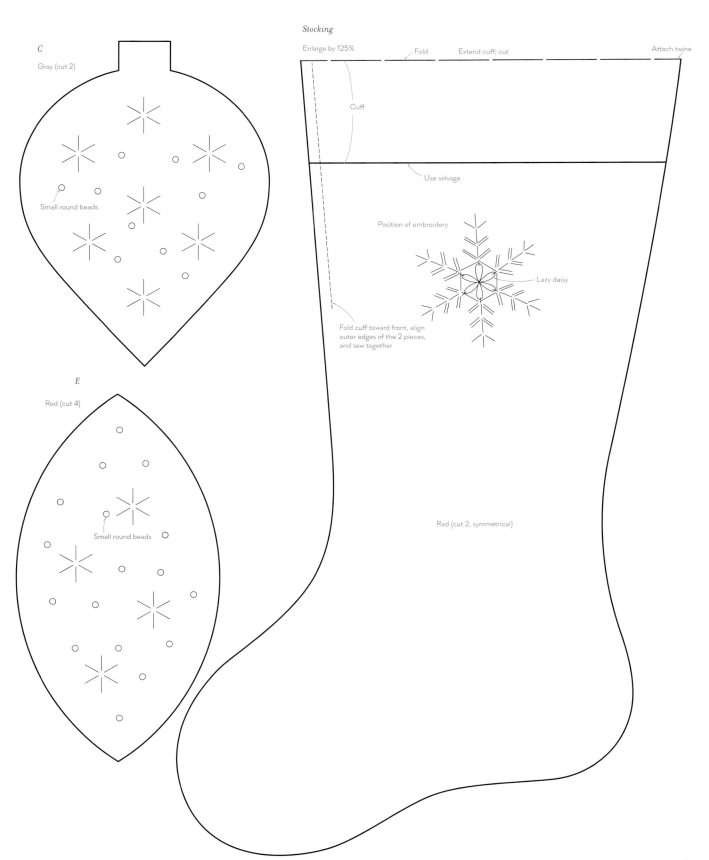

C

Gray (cut 2)

Small round beads

E

Red (cut 4)

Small round beads

Stocking

Enlarge by 125%

Fold   Extend cuff; cut   Attach twine

Cuff

Use selvage

Position of embroidery

Lazy daisy

Fold cuff toward front, align
outer edges of the 2 pieces,
and sew together

Red (cut 2, symmetrical)

 **DREAMING OF ROSES**

Materials

* Thread: [Sakuragi] DMC embroidery floss No. 25 (3733, 225, 989, 3011, 3821, 3863); DMC embroidery floss No. 5 (989)
  [Baby Betsy] DMC embroidery floss No. 25 (3733, 3731, 368, 989, 3363, 3011); DMC embroidery floss No. 5 (989)
  [Louise Odier] DMC embroidery floss No. 25 (3687, 989, 3863); DMC embroidery floss No. 5 (989); MOKUBA embroidery ribbon No. 1540, 3.5 mm wide (029)
* Fabric: Linen, off-white, 9" x 11" for each option
* Other: Fusible interfacing, 9" x 11" each; tie-dye fabric, green; double-sided fusible interfacing [Sakuragi] 4" x 2" [each] [Baby Betsy] 6" x 2" [each] [Louise Odier] 4" x 2⅜" [each]; tie-dye tulle, green, 2" square each; label plate, (1) each; ⅛"-thick styrene mounting board, 6" x 8½" each; bookbinding tape, as needed

Notes

* Finished size: 6" x 8½" each
* Apply fusible interfacing to the reverse side of the embroidery fabric before embroidering.
* Fold the fabric, and mount it on the styrene board, securing it with bookbinding tape on the back.
* Use 3 strands, unless noted otherwise.
* Use No. 25 embroidery floss, unless noted otherwise. "#5" denotes No. 5 embroidery floss.

Embroidery Pattern

(actual size)

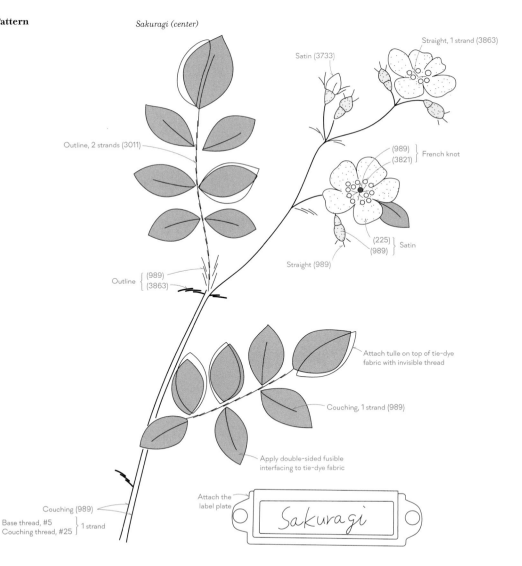

Embroidery Pattern

(actual size)

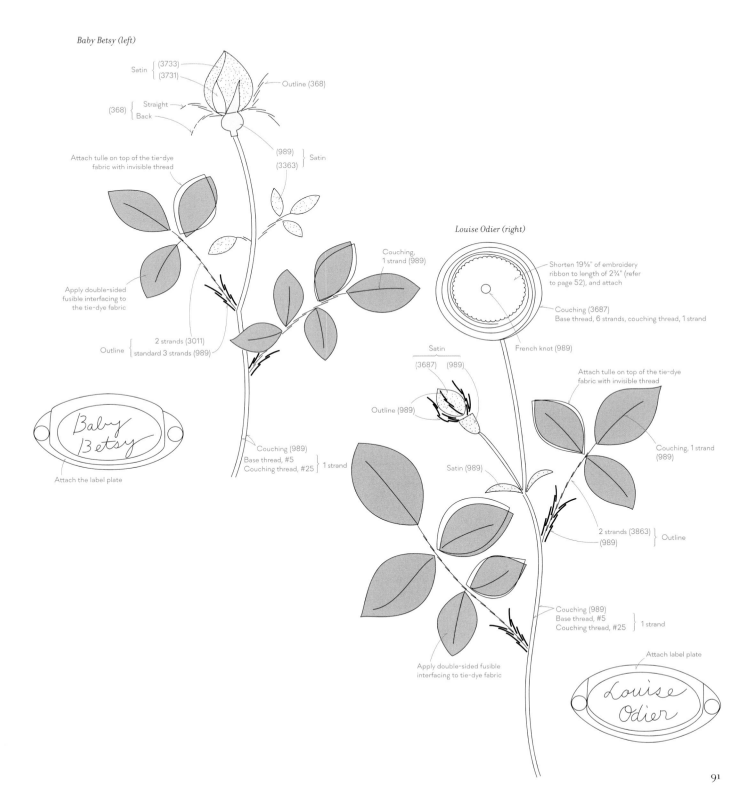

Baby Betsy (left)

Satin { (3733) (3731)

Outline (368)

(368) { Straight Back

Attach tulle on top of the tie-dye fabric with invisible thread

(989) (3363) } Satin

Couching, 1 strand (989)

Apply double-sided fusible interfacing to the tie-dye fabric

Outline { 2 strands (3011) standard 3 strands (989)

Baby Betsy

Attach the label plate

Couching (989)
Base thread, #5
Couching thread, #25 } 1 strand

Louise Odier (right)

Shorten 19⅝" of embroidery ribbon to length of 2¾" (refer to page 52), and attach

Couching (3687)
Base thread, 6 strands, couching thread, 1 strand

French knot (989)

Satin
(3687) (989)

Outline (989)

Attach tulle on top of the tie-dye fabric with invisible thread

Satin (989)

Couching, 1 strand (989)

2 strands (3863) (989) } Outline

Couching (989)
Base thread, #5
Couching thread, #25 } 1 strand

Apply double-sided fusible interfacing to tie-dye fabric

Attach label plate

Louise Odier

91

Materials

* Thread: [Viola] Kazuko Aoki Original linen thread (stem green, primrose, buttercup, campanula, charcoal, artichoke); [Ladybug] Kazuko Aoki Original linen thread (strawberry, charcoal); [Clover] Kazuko Aoki Original linen thread (stem green, leaf green); DMC embroidery floss No. 25 (ECRU)
* Fabric: Linen, white [Viola] 2⅜" x 3⅛" [Ladybug] 4" square [Clover] 4" x 5⅛"
* Other: [All] Kent paper, ivory, 8" x 5⅞"; acrylic paint, white [Viola] fusible interfacing, 2⅜" x 3⅛"; postmarked stamped envelope; ⅝"-diameter sticker seal (2) [Ladybug] fusible interfacing, 4" square; printed cotton fabric, 1⅝" x 1⅜"; postmarked stamped envelope [Clover] fusible interfacing, 4" x 5⅛"; cheesecloth, 2⅜" x 2"; postmarked stamp

Notes

* Finished size: 4" x 5⅞" [each]
* Apply fusible interfacing to the reverse side of the embroidery fabric before embroidering. Using the free-motion function, machine stitch the cheesecloth and the printed fabric to the white linen. Lightly paint with acrylic (refer to page 51), embroider the pattern, and cut it to size. Cut the Kent paper to the size specified, fold it in half, and use a quick-drying bond to attach the envelope, stamp, and fabric as shown in the diagram.
* Work satin stitch, unless noted otherwise.
* Use 1 strand of linen thread, unless noted otherwise. "#25" denotes No. 25 embroidery floss, 1 strand.

How to Make

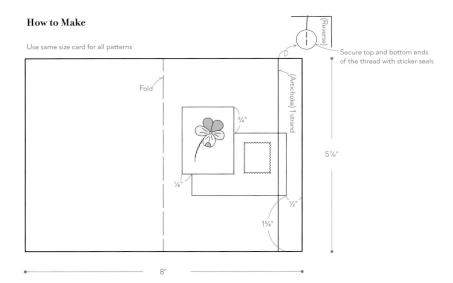

Use same size card for all patterns

(Reverse)

Secure top and bottom ends of the thread with sticker seals

Fold

(Artichoke) 1 strand

¾"

⅛"

5⅞"

½"

1⅝"

8"

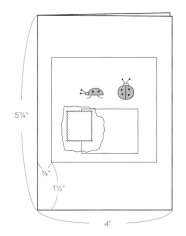

5⅞"

⅜"

1½"

4"

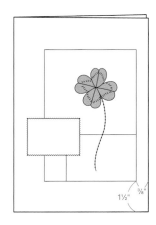

⅜"

1½"

Embroidery Pattern

(actual size)

Viola

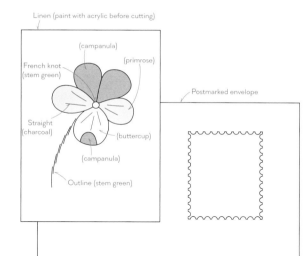

Linen (paint with acrylic before cutting)

(campanula)

(primrose)

French knot
(stem green)

Straight
(charcoal)

(buttercup)

(campanula)

Outline (stem green)

Postmarked envelope

Ladybug

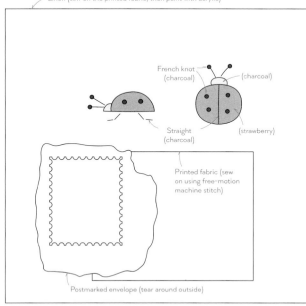

Linen (sew on the printed fabric, then paint with acrylic)

French knot
(charcoal)

(charcoal)

Straight
(charcoal)

(strawberry)

Printed fabric (sew
on using free-motion
machine stitch)

Postmarked envelope (tear around outside)

Clover

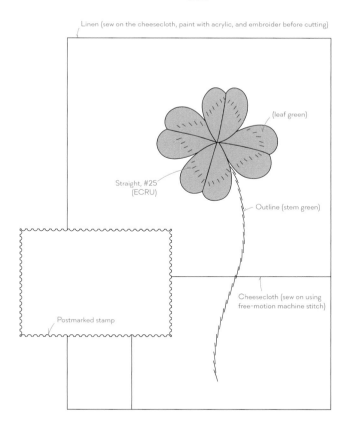

Linen (sew on the cheesecloth, paint with acrylic, and embroider before cutting)

(leaf green)

Straight, #25
(ECRU)

Outline (stem green)

Postmarked stamp

Cheesecloth (sew on using
free-motion machine stitch)

93

RESOURCES

MATERIALS

The DMC Corporation (DMC No. 25, 5, 8, Diamant Metallic)
www.dmc.com (Global Web catalog)
www.dmc-kk.com (Japan Web catalog)

Hobbyra Hobbyre (linen-blend fabric, embroidery patches)
www.hobbyra-hobbyre.com

Nihon Vogue-sha Co., Ltd. (sales agent for Kazuko Aoki Original Linen thread)
www.tezukitown.com (only ships in Japan)

REFERENCES

Field Guide to Birds, Reader's Digest
Insects of Summer, *Birds of Summer*, Fukuinkan Shoten Publishers, Inc.

ABOUT THE AUTHOR

Kazuko Aoki expresses her love for her own small garden and the flowers she cultivates there, as well as the insects and animals who visit, through the embroidery designs she creates. Using fabric as a canvas and needle and thread as her medium, her ability to skillfully craft embroidery as if she were painting a work of art has won the hearts of legions of her fans. Aoki is known for her use of unexpected materials, and many are captivated by the abundance and originality of her ideas. Her books include *An Illustrated Guide to Garden Flowers*, *Seasons of Embroidery*, and *Cross-stitch A to Z* (all published by Bunka Shuppan Kyoku), among many others.

Roost Books
An imprint Shambhala Publications, Inc.
4720 Walnut Street
Boulder, Colorado 80301
roostbooks.com

Nihon Vogue Staff Credits
Book Design: Mihoko Amano
Photography: Yukiko Tanaka, Noriaki Moriya (pages 43–52), Kazuko Aoki (pages 44–47)
Styling: Akiko Suzuki
Tracing: Satomi Dairaku (day studio)
Editorial Assistance: Fusako Kanai
Editor in charge: Akiko Taniyama

14 13 12 11 10 9 8 7 6

Printed in China

∞ This edition is printed on acid-free paper that meets the
American National Standards Institute z39.48 Standard.
♻ Shambhala Publications makes every effort to print on recycled paper.
For more information please visit www.shambhala.com.
Roost Books is distributed worldwide
by Penguin Random House, Inc., and its subsidiaries.

LIBRARY OF CONGRESS CATALOGING-IN-PUBLICATION DATA
Aoki, Kazuko, 1953– author.
[Aoki Kazuko no shishu daiari. English]
The embroidered garden: stitching through the seasons
of a flower garden/Kazuko Aoki.—First English edition.
pages   cm
Includes bibliographical references.
ISBN 978-1-61180-266-5 (pbk.: alk. paper)
1. Embroidery—Patterns. 2. Flowers in art.
3. Decoration and ornament—Plant forms. I. Title.
TT773.A6413 2015
746.44—dc23
2014030504